Dr Joan Freeman is a psychologist currently working in the Department of Education at the University of Manchester. She has been a teacher and counsellor in several schools around the country. Married to a psychiatrist, they have four grown children—three boys and then a girl.

Dr Freeman has lectured extensively in Britain and abroad on the subject of intellectual development in children, and she has appeared on numerous radio and television programmes. She directed the Gulbenkian Research Project, an in-depth study of the home and school lives of very bright children, and her book *Gifted Children* (1979) includes a description of her findings. She has published two other books and was recently awarded a Rockefeller Foundation grant to complete the editing of an international textbook on gifted children.

Clever Children

A Parent's Guide

Dr Joan Freeman

Foreword by H. J. Eysenck

Hamlyn Paperbacks

CLEVER CHILDREN
ISBN 0 600 20345 X

First published in Great Britain 1983
by Hamlyn Paperbacks

Copyright © 1983 by Dr Joan Freeman

Hamlyn Paperbacks are published by
The Hamlyn Publishing Group Ltd,
Astronaut House, Feltham,
Middlesex, England

Printed and bound in Great Britain by
Cox & Wyman Ltd. Reading

Contents

Foreword

Many people are discouraged when they hear that intelligence
is to a large extent determined by genetic factors, and that
environment does not contribute very much to the final
product. While this is a true statement based on large-scale
experimental and statistical research on countless twins,
families, adopted children etc., the conclusion needs
interpretation in order to be meaningful. The very term
'intelligence' has at least three distinguishable meanings,
labelled by psychologists as intelligence A, intelligence B,
and intelligence C. To understand the differences between
these is the beginning of wisdom in relation to the interpretation of scientific findings for practical usefulness.

Intelligence A is the biological, genetic basis of all
intellectual differences between the bright and the dull, the
gifted and the retarded, the genius and the idiot. Intelligence
B, on the other hand, is the intelligence shown in everyday
life, in school, at university, in one's job, in adjusting to
society, and quite generally in day-to-day living. Intelligence
C is, again, something different; it is the IQ or intelligence
quotient, as measured by typical intelligence tests.
Intelligence C aims to come as close as possible to
intelligence A and to intelligence B, but of course, while
reasonably successful, it is far from a perfect measure.

It is intelligence A that is genetically determined; insofar
as intelligence C, i.e. the IQ test, is successful in measuring
intelligence A, IQ too is largely determined by genetic
factors. But intelligence B, the kind of successful adjustment
a person makes to the demands of society, is probably
determined by many factors additional to intelligence A, and
is only imperfectly measured by intelligence C.

The situation is rather similar to our measurement of

heat. This began with people recognizing differences in the sensations produced by putting their hands in snow, or bringing them near a fire. Gradually the understanding of heat became more refined, and measurement through thermometers became possible. We now define heat in terms of thermometer readings, but this is analogous to intelligence A, and might be called heat A. There is, also, heat B, i.e. heat (or cold) as experienced by people in everyday life circumstances. We know that the so-called 'chill factor' is very important in whether one feels or does not feel the cold; this chill factor is simply the amount of wind present which blows away the envelope of heated air that surrounds us all. Then there is humidity; heat feels much worse when the air is humid than when it is dry. These and many other factors are additional to 'heat A', and they determine what our actual reactions to a given situation will be, i.e. whether we put on additional clothes, or put on the air conditioning, or what. From the scientific point of view heat A is of course important, but from the point of view of adjusting one's behaviour to the actual circumstances of one's life, it is heat B that counts. Heat C, of course, is the actual thermometer measurement of the molecular movements that are the physical reality underlying our experience of heat and, while closely related to heat A, it is certainly not a perfect monitor.

While there is little that we can do at the moment to influence intelligence A, we can do a lot to influence intelligence B, i.e. the actual use to which intelligence A is put by a given person. It has been demonstrated dramatically that some people with very high IQs adjust very poorly, perhaps for emotional reasons; they are neurotic, stand in their own light, suffer from examination anxieties and other phobias, and never reach the level of success in life which corresponds to their high intelligence. Others fail because they were not sufficiently motivated to do the hard work needed to translate high innate intelligence into achievement. Indeed, there are many reasons why a person of high intelligence may not be successful.

Dr Joan Freeman's book is devoted to telling parents how they can best help their children to achieve the optimum level of intellectual development, commensurate with their innate abilities. Such advice is very necessary because most parents, although quite capable of dealing with all the usual problems of upbringing, are not aware of the special problems presented by clever children. They are the seed corn of society, and no society can long survive which does not lay particular stress on the advancement of these children. Hence the social and practical importance of books like this one; no one is in a better position than parents to help their children along the difficult road from giftedness to achievement, and the sage advice that Dr Freeman has distilled from countless scientific investigations into common sense and understandable counsel will prove immensely useful to parents lucky enough to have one or more clever children!

Professor H. J. Eysenck

Introduction

Parenting is an art, and all artists need to develop their sensitivity. Much of this book is devoted to helping parents improve theirs. For there has never been a better time to be a clever child. Ability is at a premium, and parents are undoubtedly the best-placed people to help their children reach their potential. Bright children born to loving, concerned and knowledgeable parents have the finest chance to develop their minds with the greatest pleasure and success. The pursuit of excellence is a choice available to everyone, from all walks of life. Every child wants to be good at something, and every child can be.

The psychological foundations for learning begin to be laid at birth and are already becoming firm by the time a child is three years old, though of course there is still plenty of time for mental growth after that. Even though no single method of bringing up children can be sure to work, even for children in the same family, some methods do seem to be more worthwhile than others, and many of the best are set out in this book.

Probably the most effective way parents can help their children is through forming a close relationship with them from the day they are born. That very early closeness is the cradle of a lively intelligence which lasts for life. Although babies develop basic skills (such as reaching out for things) without help, their parents can encourage them to enjoy experimenting with their new learning. Even for a tiny baby, variety is the spice of life.

The deep pleasure which these adventures in early learning can give a baby will do a lot to help him feel good about learning in general. This will go on working for him as he discovers his own special strengths and interests. Doing the right thing with your baby at the right time will always give him greater confidence and an easier educational climb than he could ever have managed without your help.

With such a good start in family life, the next stage (which soon begins to matter to teachers, too) is the finer, practical detail of guiding the intellectual progress of clever children. How should this be done? Will they be better or worse off if they are treated differently from other children? Does cleverness have an effect on a child's personality? Though the list of questions is long, the key to the answers is always in the child herself. No two children are alike and parents are the vital initiators in spotting and promoting each one's individual cleverness. If you can enhance your child's native ability by encouraging her sense of self-worth, then that will form the basis of her competence and a lifelong ability to make use of the gifts she was born with.

One of the most welcome benefits of the interest taken in clever chidren, both at home and at school, is the effect this has on other children. It encourages extra respect for all children's abilities and a willingness to search for the best a child can do. This can bring about a general rise in the level of parents' and teachers' expectations, to which the children often respond very favourably. In schools where clever children are catered for and all the children feel important and valuable, teaching takes on a fresh sparkle.

I have chosen to use 'he' or 'she' more or less alternately in describing babies and children. The reason for this is simply because that is the way they are born – more or less alternately as boys and girls. As parents too come in both sexes, I have only referred to the mother or father specifically where this is important. In general I am writing about activities and relationships between parents and children which apply equally, whoever is doing the parenting.

This book offers a positive psychological approach to children's intellectual development, one very much more concerned with 'dos' than 'don'ts'. It contains very little about what your child *should* be doing at any particular age –

clever children do not always stick to the rules anyway. Instead it is a wide collection of research-based knowledge about how children's minds develop and work, with practical suggestions as to how parents can help them along. The ideas gathered here are valuable for every child.

You will find that as you become more familiar with this positive approach it will become a habit, encouraging you to keep on thinking constructively. You and your children will be better able to grow together, learning from each other. Perhaps the greatest joy in parenting is what you learn from your children. With their free unshackled minds they can lead you into areas of interest which you did not even know existed before. Mine certainly did.

In developing my ideas I have had immeasurable assistance from the careful, painstaking work of countless child psychologists who have described their scientific research in academic journals and books. What I have been able to do, as an academic myself, is to search long and hard through the statistics (and sometimes the jargon) to translate what they have discovered into practicable, everyday ideas. I have acknowledged some of these sources in the text and indexed them by number in the Reference section at the back of the book.

In addition to these descriptions of evidence from around the world, I have also included aspects of the four-year Gulbenkian research project on clever children which I directed in the North of England, in which I was primarily concerned to find out why some children were recognized as clever while others (of equal ability) were not. It emerged that children's cleverness was sometimes judged as much by their behaviour as by their intellectual ability. This meant that quiet, undemanding clever children sometimes missed out on the attention they needed, particularly when they were very young. Close contact with these very bright children, their families and schools showed me that those who made the greatest progress in developing their potential tended to come from the most educationally positive homes, where they received the mental freedom, encouragement and opportunity they needed – whatever their abilities. This research is described in much more detail in my book *Gifted Children*. The children and their parents who took part in the project have taught me more than they knew, and I thank them sincerely.

I would also like to express my appreciation to the many people – parents, teachers, academics and students – who have spent time discussing clever children with me while I have been writing this book. It has always been worthwhile to hear their comments and responses, and to compare their experiences with my own.

The famous child psychiatrist Donald Winnicott once said that you don't have to be a perfect parent – just good enough. This thought has given me comfort over the years of my own children's upbringing. I pass his words on to you with the sincere hope that you too will find great pleasure in the time you share with your children.

Dr Joan Freeman

Chapter 1

THE CLEVER ONES

The world needs clever children – those whose potential capabilities could contribute greatly to life in many fields of endeavour, if they're given the chance to develop. The clever child may be yours or mine, whether we are rich or poor, whatever our race, and wherever we live. At least half a million children, one in ten of all the children in Great Britain, are born clever enough to make them outstanding in some way.

What people call cleverness depends, to some extent, on their own point of view and on the life they lead. For example, the clever cave-boy would probably have been the best prospective hunter. In ancient Greece, the clever child would have been noticed for his logical thinking, clear speech and sporting ability. At the turn of this century, clever children were those who could recite long passages from memory – clearly and with expression – or write columns of figures in long straight lines: in those days, hard work, obeying all the rules and coming top of the class were the mark of a clever child. Robert Graves, the poet, in his autobiography *Goodbye to All That*, described how his father pulled him out of school when he found his son crying over a 23-times multiplication table. He also recalled having to do mental arithmetic to the rhythm of a metronome.

It's not only the end product but also the quality of performance and a lively imagination which thread through all notable achievement, most obviously in the arts but just as powerfully in the sciences. Einstein was very bored in his German grammar school, where he was expected to reproduce what he'd been taught, and he didn't do at all well in exams. Then, when his uncle taught him how to use his imagination with numbers, he went on to change the world of mathematics and physics. But Einstein was a genius, one of those rare people who bring new ideas into being which can change people's way of looking at life.

Geniuses are usually thought of as rather more than just clever: they're truly great people who leave their society and perhaps even humankind a little different because of their contribution. Beethoven, Isaac Newton, Picasso and Marie Curie were all geniuses. Even as little children they often showed unusually strong interest in the specific subject areas which later came to dominate their lives, sometimes to the exclusion of most other things. In a study of eminent scientists in America in the 1950s, Anne Roe[1] found that early in childhood her scientists-to-be had made serious adult-like collections and had performed experiments. Handel was composing at the age of eleven, Mozart at four and Mendelssohn at nine. Alexander Pope had had poems published by the age of twelve and Robert Burns by fourteen. Henry Ford started as a watch repairman so young that his employers found it better for him not to be seen at work. Genius implies a very superior ability to be original, to push back the frontiers of knowledge and ideas, and this ability often becomes apparent very early in life.

This book is written for the parents of children who are notably brighter than the average in some way, but the great majority of them will never be considered geniuses. Most parents of clever children to whom I've spoken, very understandably, want their children to lead a happy, normal life. So I've brought together my experience as a teacher, psychologist, researcher and parent to help other parents understand and help their normal, clever children to do their best and be happy. Parents are the best resources a clever child has, since they are the most sensitive to her needs and concerned about her future.

Children's normal intellectual development
Psychologists are never happy about committing themselves to saying exactly what a child ought to be doing at any

particular age. This is because there is considerable variation between individual children's patterns of development. Both psychologically and physically a child may grow in spurts with rests in between, or keep on growing steadily. Every child has his own individual tempo and style of development, as personal as his face.

Still, in order to decide whether their child is clever or not, most parents want some understanding of normal development in children. But it is important to realize that *what is called normal really means average.* The normal development levels are averages taken from studies of thousands of children of the same age. But these averages can change over the years with changing conditions, and they're not easily transferable from one nation to another (such as between America and Britain). Bearing all this in mind, what follows is a rough outline of the sort of advancement you can expect in a 'normal' child's mental development. (There's more detail about the way the mind works in Chapter 3.)

Using words

From birth a baby will listen and respond to words and signs. By a year old she will have learned to produce a few words herself, like 'Mama' and 'Dada', and in between trying them out, she practises her new talking skills by babbling. Most babies can usually manage a few short sentences by the time they are two years old, though researchers are agreed that girls are normally more advanced than boys in the use of words. Wide-ranging research in America directed by Eleanor Maccoby[2] has shown that not only do girls say their first word earlier, but they go on to talk properly earlier. Boys usually (but not always) catch up in later childhood. You could count up the number of words your child has to see how well she's getting on, though late talking doesn't automatically mean slow mental development, either now or in the future. Winston Churchill didn't talk until he was three years old.

Learning to talk is affected by a number of things in a child's life, such as his need to communicate by that parti-

17

cular means. For example, if as a parent you manage well enough to anticipate your baby's needs for food and drink in response to his gestures, then he might be a little slow in getting round to asking for them by name. This doesn't matter in the long run. Learning to talk is linked to emotion too, so that children who have had upsets in their lives – perhaps moving house or a change in the people who look after them – may suffer a setback in talking. The way children feel about words also affects the way they use them and the thoughts that are sparked off by words. But this is very hard to pinpoint specifically, and in fact it's true for adults too. Most of these feelings are buried deep in our unconscious minds; we're not aware of the way we talk and think – we just get on with it.

Using numbers

It may be hard to believe, but future computational skills have their roots in the first year of life. By the time she's a year old a baby can put one brick on top of another on a smooth firm surface. In this way she begins to glimpse the basic arithmetical idea of 'more than'; 'less than' will come later, at about two years old. An average three-year-old can usually count to five, and by four years old to ten. But a real understanding of numbers only comes after they are memorized. To a toddler the number four is not the abstract idea of the cipher 4 that older children understand. But by the age of three a toddler can usually cope with ideas of 'enoughness', which is somewhere between saying the numbers and understanding them. You could try asking your toddler 'Have I put enough cups on the table for tea?' to see what stage she's reached.

By the time she's five years old a child should be able to add up numbers under five, and by six years she can not only add up numbers under ten, but can subtract numbers under five. Boys and girls seem to develop at an even pace in arithmetical skills, but boys often do better on spatial skills, which show in making patterns and understanding how things work.

18

Using experience

Some kinds of mental development need experience to work on. The idea of time, for example, calls for the exercise of memories of past events and some language ability. Toddlers can usually begin to plan ahead with the idea of time by about three years old. They can then use something they know well, such as bedtime or teatime, to plan around.

Unlike adults, little children have yet to accumulate enough experience to imagine how to cope with some new situations. A baby, for example, has to learn from many demonstrations that Daddy's face is going to appear again over the top of the sofa when they're playing peek-a-boo. Later on, the game loses its excitement when the baby knows he's crouching down there all the time. At about a year old a crawling baby can watch you put a toy under a cushion and he'll 'find' it again. But if you pretend to put it under one cushion and sneak it under another one instead, he'll still only look under the first, as he hasn't enough experience to realize that if it's not under one, it may be under another. He should be able to cope with more than one hiding place, though, by the time he's eighteen months old.

A little child also needs experience before she can learn to reason. It takes at least three years to work up a recognizable level of argument which involves responses and not just statements of opinion. By five years old a child is usually able to draw sensible conclusions and to discuss the differences and similarities between what she sees. Christopher Robin, you may remember, saw that Nanny's dressing gown 'was a beautiful blue, but it hasn't a hood. Mine has a hood' when he was about five years old.

Sometimes little ones lack the experience and knowledge of life which they need to reach the 'right' conclusions, such as when a toddler wants to marry Mummy or Daddy when he or she grows up. They may jump to conclusions without working things out carefully enough, either because they're lazy or because they're so quick that they don't negotiate the slower paths of reasoning, but instead jump ahead to the logically right (but practically incorrect) solutions. Taking his clue from adults, one of our children used to get a 'heggache' in his tummy when he was small; nothing wrong with his thinking and fortunately easy to understand.

Using letters

Sometime during toddlerhood children discover that making scribbles on paper is a way of expressing their thoughts. Then, through copying shapes and drawing pictures, many children can shape some letters by the time they are four. But most usually start doing this at school when they are five. Reading and writing progress often goes together in the beginning, though when children really love reading, their writing can lag behind.

Most children learn to read when they go to school and can manage simple books like Dick Bruna's by the end of their first year. Some clever children seem to teach themselves to read by absorbing words from all around them such as those on cereal packets, road signs and record labels. A clever child will probably recognize that D R W H O means 'Dr Who' by the age of three and may recognize his own name if you print it out in big letters, depending on how difficult a name it is.

The age by which children learn to use letters in reading and writing depends a lot on the encouragement and assistance they receive at home. If you, as a parent, enjoy using words yourself, then you can expect that your child will too.

How to spot a clever toddler

Now that I've briefly covered 'average' mental development, here is a short outline of some features of a clever toddler's behaviour which will help you to judge whether or not your child is clever. Judging cleverness in little babies is much more difficult than in toddlers, so I've devoted the whole of the next chapter to a discussion of that subject.

The old physical milestones of when a child first sits up, crawls, stands up or walks are not now seen as such certain indicators of cleverness as they once were. Mental characteristics are really a much better guide, though they're not entirely reliable as children can change incredibly quickly. Remember that clever children are just as different from one another as any other group of children – some may be lively, into everything and very friendly, while others can be shy and prefer to keep to themselves. So *use this list with caution: it's only meant as a guide.*

Lively minds

The most noticeable feature of clever children is the liveliness of their minds, which comes across in many ways, especially their delight with words. They're very 'talkative' little babies, but their babbling and cooing soon give way to a stream of toddler conversation which can become quite serious, even by the age of three. Many of them are reading by four years old and then they seem to devour every word in sight. Clever children can have prodigious memories, even in babyhood, and certainly by the time they're into their third year. For instance, a child might remember going on a picnic a year before. Parents of clever children often remark on their toddlers' amazing memories. They can also concentrate for hours when very small if they're interested in something.

Many clever children seem to be born with a keen edge of competitive spirit. They may compete against themselves, always trying to do better next time, or they may compete against other children in the sense of (as the song says) 'Anything you can do, I can do better'. Does your toddler try to succeed over and over again, showing great perseverance until she does?

Even as toddlers, clever children are usually very quick to spot tiny differences and catch on to unusual associations between ideas. But toddlers still don't know very much about the world they live in, as this conversation shows: *Toddler:* 'You can't built houses on hills.' *Mother:* 'Yes you can, look at the houses going up that hill.' *Toddler:* 'But how can the floors be flat then?' *Mother:* 'Well, you either have to dig the house into the hill or let is stick out like a balcony.'

Toddler (trying to keep her end up in the conversation): 'I think you should build houses "properly", even if the floors would be slanting; you know, just put them on the hill. People could go up and down inside. It would save a lot of trouble.'

Awareness

Some clever toddlers can use their very high level of awareness to take in information very quickly, sometimes before you reach the end of your sentence and sometimes from more than one source at a time, such as listening to two conversations and getting full measure from both. There are adults who feel that they can do this too, but their way of going about it is different – they alternate attention and memory. They put a little of what they've heard into store, then return to it when they've heard the next bit, mentally jumping back and forth to keep the two inputs open, but actually only paying attention to one of them at a time. Clever children, on the other hand, can sometimes take in two sets of information and process them simultaneously. There may be times when you're surprised to find that your toddler had heard every word of your conversation and that he can also repeat exactly what he heard on the radio at the same time.

Their heightened awareness often allows clever toddlers to imagine what it's like to be another person. This means that they're pretty good at copying other people's behaviour and learning fast from the experience. Unfortunately this can give them the appearance of being quite grown-up and it is easily mistaken for the genuine maturity which they will grow into later.

It often happens that clever children are also highly sensitive. There is a theory that this sensitivity allows the child to be so bright in the first place, by enabling him to absorb a wide variety of information and ideas which less able children might miss. But sometimes that extra sensitivity may make it hard for him to bear even normal adult criticism, taking it too much to heart. Clever toddlers are usually responsive to gentle guidance rather than punishment, and they need praise just as much as any other children.

Ability to learn

By ten months or so a clever baby should be quite sociable in an almost adult way. She should be able to get hold of your attention and keep it when she wants it. For example, a clever one-year-old may have learned that she's going to get further by being charming than by screaming for attention. So she may play with her half-learned new words with a smile for your delight, seeming to know that it will make you want to stay and enjoy her success.

Clever children seem to have a particularly keen appetite for learning so that when they're given the opportunity to learn, they grab it. As they get older, their knowledge becomes wider and deeper than that of other children so that, for example, a six-year-old may have the knowledge of a nine-year-old and thus seem even cleverer than he really is. It's not that he's getting more clever all the time, it just looks that way. Parents may well wonder where clever children get all their knowledge from; they seem to absorb it from television, books, other people's conversations and so on.

I was giving an intelligence test to Millicent a couple of years ago. As she was only five, I hadn't bothered to conceal the test manual on my knees under the table as you're supposed to. She was obviously doing very well, especially when it came to the point where she had to repeat seven numbers back to me. 'I think I should tell you' she piped 'that I can read upside down.'

Independence

Clever toddlers have a sureness about what they do. They are comfortable with themselves and take pride in their accomplishments. Sometimes they even try to dominate their parents, mischievously thinking of ways to play tricks and have fun, such as hiding Daddy's shoes when he's about to go out. Or they may want to outshine their parents – go them one better. Once I was making an arrangement to meet someone over the phone. 'How about Saturday afternoon?' I asked. 'I'm free.' To which my clever toddler responded proudly: 'I'm free and a half.'

Even in their first few days at school, clever children are usually outstandingly independent and competent at their lessons. Some develop special interests they want to follow up in depth, even while they are only at nursery school, so that by the time they reach the infants, they're really beginning to know their way around the subject. William, for example, loved classical music, and had some records which he could play as he wanted; he was very careful with them. But his reading, aged four, was still a bit wobbly on such names as Prokofiev and Tchaikovsky, so he remembered numbers for the pieces instead. One day, while out shopping with his mother, he heard something he recognized over the supermarket loudspeaker 'Oh listen!' he cried in rapture, 'It's number 27.'

Keeping a diary

Obviously, deciding whether your child is clever, and if so how and when to give her special attention, requires careful observation. It may sound like a bit of a chore, but it can be very helpful to keep a diary. Often when you put something in writing it helps you take a step outside the hurly-burly of everyday living so that you can get a clearer, more objective view of what is happening in your family. Then, looking back, you may be able to see how situations have developed. A diary will not only help you to judge whether you have a clever child – for example, whether she was always intellectually advanced for her age – but, of equal importance, it will help you to watch her emotional development. As intellectual and emotional development are tied together, they should be watched together.

Your record book doesn't have to be a proper printed diary and you don't even have to write in it regularly: simply keep it handy, so that you can jot down things as they happen or when you particularly feel like it. A small notebook is perfect, preferably with a hard cover so that it will last well through many readings, and maybe several children, over the years. It may be the best book you've ever read.

There are three aspects of diary-keeping which you should bear in mind when you're writing about your child's development – progress, feelings and plans. When you write, try to think through the events that occur, rather than just keeping a record. For example, instead of writing: 'Mary's back teeth through. Bill [husband] away this week', try to make your entry more like this: 'Mary's back teeth showing with much crying. Bill's been away a week now – is it pain she's crying for, or can she be missing him? I am; can I be passing my misery on to poor Mary? I'll keep closer to her and take her out for a change of scene this afternoon.'

The interpretation you choose to give to the events in your life is up to you: it's your opinion which counts in your family and, after all, diaries are private.

Try to take a long view of your child's development, both when you're writing and when you're reading through your diary. It can help you to see changing patterns in his development. Perhaps you will be able to see how right you were when you thought Richard was trying to talk at six months old and you were pooh-poohed, or maybe his early self-confidence took a dip when he started school. A diary can help you to see things in perspective and maybe spot potential problems before they have a chance to become difficult. After some years you might find you have built up a useful series of entries, like the following ones about how Sarah started learning to read.

Eight months old: Showed Sarah the pictures in her board book. She reached out for it and showed real interest. Am very excited, so's Robert. Mother says Sarah's far too young to read still.

One year and two months: Sarah can turn the pages of her new cloth book and frowns over the pictures. She pretends to

25

be reading; well, I think so. Lots of fun, we laugh a lot. It gives her great pleasure.

Three years and four months: Now she can read a few words Sarah seems very keen to learn more. She's driving me mad with 'What's this and this?' I can't cope with her demands and those of the new baby. Sometimes I can give her the hug I know she needs, but sometimes I seem so cross nowadays.

Four years old: Sarah's started nursery school. Feel great relief, but she screamed the place down. Should have prepared her better. Robert's work has let up a bit, so he'll spend more time with her. Wish I could too.

Five years old: Proper school, but Sarah doesn't seem very keen. Teacher says she's clever, but won't try. Worried. Robert and I will give her a lot of love and support every day. She really needs us now.

Six years old: Sarah on an even course at school: glad I kept a diary.

From time to time, describe a typical day in the life of your child. Does it seem balanced to you? Does she have to spend all the time doing things which only interest you, with little alternative? Perhaps you could offer her a little more choice. Are you providing enough praise and encouragement to build up her confidence to explore? Find out what children usually do at this age; you could discover that your expectations are too high and such knowledge could avoid an imminent collision between your expectations and her achievement. Your diary is really your personal textbook of your child's total development. Try to develop a feeling for her character at the same time as watching out for any special talents.

You think your child may be clever

It's not always pure pleasure to realize you may be the parent of a clever child. There are a few worrying ideas about clever children which pop up in newspapers and conversations from time to time. Here I've put together some answers to questions which parents often ask me about their clever children.

Do they need special attention?
In general, clever children learn faster and perform better than the average child, so it may appear as though they can do without special attention. But whether this is really so depends partly on your view of education. If you think every child should have the same education, then clever children can be ignored, as they'll probably get on well enough, and the most attention should go to those who need help in keeping up. But if you think every child should be educated to his full potential, then clever children will also need their fair share of attention in order to achieve that. (The educational needs of clever children are described in more detail in Chapter 8.)

I believe that all children – including the clever ones – have a right to find their education interesting and challenging. They shouldn't be bound by such learning restrictions as keeping to an average pace all the time, so they will need some special opportunities to suit their extra ability to learn. If a clever child is wasting much of his energy in unnecessary activity, such as learning simple stages of maths when his mind is capable of jumping some of them, he can be put off maths by the sheer drudgery of it in his most formative years.

Before education became obligatory for all children, some clever children were educated by tutors, or in small groups, which does not normally happen today. Mozart, for example, had personal tutors from a very early age, as well as his father's help. He would be unlikely to have had the time he needed to develop his talent for musical composition in the hurly-burly of a big school. Still, you never know; Benjamin Britten's aunt used to make him stop composing when bedtime came. 'If it's any good,' she would say, 'it'll wait till morning.'

Should we tell the school?

Parents are the most likely people to spot a clever child; after all, they've had longer than anyone else to get to know their child. Sometimes parents judge their child's cleverness by watching her play with other children and noticing how she's ahead of them in, say, asking more penetrating questions or discovering how to do things more quickly. But there are times when parents just feel it in their bones, as a sort of hunch, and this should be investigated to find out for sure.

Parents are often worried about seeming 'pushy' if they tell the teacher what they feel about their child's ability, but they have a responsibility to their child to be honest with her teacher. If the teacher and the parents aren't working along the same lines, the child is the loser. The chances are very good that a school will do its best to co-operate with parents if they show a genuine concern to work along with the teachers, rather than just appearing to claim special attention for *their* child. It's helpful to the school (and themselves) if parents list their evidence of the child's cleverness before they present the idea to the school. Note down pre-school reading, early talking, unusual words or ideas, musical talent and so on.

How will they cope with life?

As they get older, clever children broaden their interests more and more, so that as well as being better than other children at school subjects, they may also have a much wider range of interests outside school. They're often particularly interested in music, for example, and will gladly give up free time to take part in rehearsals of orchestras and choirs. Many clever children seem to be good at everything from maths to art, from sport to philosophy. Though it's hard for parents to cope with such a wide range of excellence, it's very exciting too.

Parents may worry that clever children are trying too many things, over-extending and thereby exhausting themselves. But if a child is choosing his activities freely, rather than being pushed into them by an adult, there's little danger of that happening. What may seem like work to an adult may be fun to a child. Some clever children, though, settle for one thing at a time, learning everything they can about it until they're satisfied . . . and then dropping it. Our eldest son, for instance, worked intensely through jigsaw puzzles, making puppet plays and steam trains before he got on to pipe organs, and he is now studying the trombone at music college.

Clever children can be quite bossy in group games, since they often feel they understand the rules better than the others. This behaviour doesn't make them popular, so they are more likely to turn to athletics or non-competitive sports. It sometimes happens that clever children are among the youngest in their class. This can be because they've been jumped a year, or because they started school a year early. Teachers may forget that the clever child is as young as he is, so he appears to others to be small for his age. This is especially true for boys in secondary schools. Remind yourself and your child that, if he appears to be undersized, it's really because he's a whole year younger than the others. But it can still be hard for a child to live with, and moving up a class isn't always worth it.

Does cleverness in children last?

The question of 'early ripe – early rot?' is often asked of children who are advanced for their years. To some people, it seems positively unhealthy to be clever in childhood; as Shakespeare wrote in *Richard III*: 'So wise so young, they say, do never live long'. But that idea is quite untrue today. For every Chopin, Shelley or Brontë who died before their time, there are many more Menuhins, Ted Hughes or Somerset Maughams who have lived to a ripe old age. The precocious children who died young were born into an age when medicine was less effective, and their less clever contemporaries risked the same fate of a premature death.

On the whole, clever children do turn out to be pretty

bright adults. However, with those who end up as merely average, the likelihood is that they were unusually advanced at the time they were noticed and have returned to their own normal state as they grow. It's a bit like height; a girl may stand out head and shoulders above the others of her age until she reaches adolescence, when she stops growing. As all the others continue to grow, they catch up with her and perhaps even pass her. It's impossible for parents to judge whether their child will always be ahead of others, either in height or in mental ability. All you can do is fit her up as comfortably as you can at the time, both in her clothes and her education.

Who are the gifted children?

These are the cleverest of clever children – say, the top two per cent of all children. Their abilities are such as to make them quite outstanding. That is not to say that giftedness is always obvious; no matter what their abilities, all children can run into problems which prevent them from doing their best. Gifted children may be denied opportunities for learning if they do not have access to appropriate equipment or teaching, such as a violin and a violin teacher. They can have emotional problems too, just like other children, for example if there is trouble at home, and this can get in the way of their learning progress.

Parents usually have a good idea of how bright their children are, as I found in the course of my research in the North of England (described on page 153 and in detail in my book *Gifted Children*[3]). But they hesitate to use the word 'gifted'; perhaps it sounds a bit like boasting. It is just a description, though, which indicates extremely high ability in either a general or a specific area. Some children are remarkably good at almost everything, but others may have precise aptitudes for certain subjects such as fine art or gymnastics. Whatever it is, gifted children need plenty of help to develop their talents. Most gifted children can't make the most of themselves, or rise to the top like cream, without any help. They need expert tuition and provision for learning to develop their full potential.

Whatever their special abilities, or however deeply they may think, gifted children are normally happy and healthy. You couldn't pick one out in a crowd, for they do not look any different from other children. I did get the impression in my research, though, that they have a more penetrating gaze!

This book is concerned with a wider range of clever children than those who are gifted; roughly the top ten per cent of all children. However, this does include gifted children and so what is written here applies equally to them.

Chapter 2

YOUR AMAZING BABY

Only very recently, beginning about twenty years ago, have psychologists taken a real interest in newborn babies and made careful scientific observations of them. For centuries it had been thought that at birth a baby was just, in the philosopher John Locke's words, a *tabula rasa* – a clean slate on which parents had merely to 'write' correctly in order to bring up a perfect child. In contrast, the French philosopher Jean Jacques Rousseau believed that the child was born wise – a 'noble savage' – and, if left to develop naturally, would become a moral and knowledgeable adult. From the newborn baby's point of view the world was, in the words of the 19th-century psychologist William James, just 'a blooming buzzing confusion'. On that basis, parents were advised to guard their babies from disturbance such as bright lights or spicy foods, since these would only add to their confusion. Be warned that some of this feeling that the baby must be kept unstimulated at all times still persists – a situation which produces bored babies.

Later, in this century, babies' daily lives became so rigidly ordered that even the newborn had to be taught to 'behave' – to be hungry on command (four-hourly) and to cry at appropriate times (just before feeding). Much of this feeling about babies lasted until Dr Benjamin Spock loosened the reins in the 1950s.

By patient study, psychologists have now accumulated enough evidence to show clearly that babies are neither blank sheets nor like army recruits. Instead, they come ready supplied with a whole set of personal characteristics, and most excitingly, a will to find things out. How they progress in their early discoveries, though, is very dependent on the attitudes, understanding and knowledge of those who look after them. As this is usually (but not always) the mother, I shall refer to her as the baby's earliest care-giver.

Where cleverness beings

The making of a clever child can be said to begin even before conception. Although there's not much that prospective parents can do about their ancestry and the genetic characteristics they are passing on, they *can* be effective in giving a good home start to the next generation.

Perhaps the single most important event in a child's life is her parents' decision to have a baby. A truly wanted baby has the advantage of starting life with positive feelings from both parents about bringing up children. These babies are usually easier to bring up and have less colic than unwanted babies. But these positive, welcoming feelings are not always found when the conception was a 'mistake'. Not very long ago – before the pill and other reliable forms of contraception were widely available, to be precise – there was always the risk that making love would result in another human coming to live on the earth for at least the next half century. Now, for most of us, there is a good chance that future generations will be wanted and prepared for, well before they're born.

Any woman's health and habits can, of course, have undesirable side-effects on her unborn child. For example, cigarette smoke, whether from the mother's own cigarettes or from a smokey atmosphere, has been found to lower the newborn's birth weight. This in turn can lower his resistance to illness and may mean that he does not thrive as he should. Children whose mothers smoked heavily (20-30 cigarettes a day) when pregnant have been found to have more difficulties at school and are more likely to be overactive. Alcohol, too, even as little as an ounce a day, has been found to affect the newborn baby's liveliness. Pregnant women who drank very heavily have been found to have low birth weight babies who were less well coordinated in their movements, sluggish and hard to arouse. The conclusion is simple and the evidence is there: cut out the poisonous drugs of nicotine and alcohol, at least while you are pregnant.

Good food and exercise are greatly beneficial to mothers-to-be and their babies. But it is only when the diet is really poor, such as happens in times of famine or prolonged poverty, that the baby's abilities are likely to be permanently affected by lack of nourishment before birth. Older women (over thirty-five years) do face an increased risk of having a backward child, though this risk is decreased if the father is younger. Good antenatal care is freely available in Britain, and all the risks are enormously reduced for those who take advantage of it.

A much more difficult problem for parents is how to ensure that the baby is born as perfectly as it has grown in the womb. Although it shouldn't be so, the quality of the maternity services can vary from distict to district and some areas of the country have better facilities than others. It is possible to find out the kind of provision available in different areas, and you may then be able to arrange to have your baby in an area or hospital with the best newborn health records. This could, at the very worst, make a difference between life and death, or it could simply be a matter of having the facilities available to take swift action if necessary to prevent even the slightest damage at birth.

The best possible birth

Sometimes, as a result of deep psychological probing or under hypnosis, people say they remember what it felt like before they were born. They mostly tell of the cosiness of the womb, and describe how terrible it was when they were struggling and being pushed out. It's only possible to accept these stories at their face value for, although they may well be true, they may also come from the imagination or from half-memories of what adults know of birth. Some of these stories, though, are found across the world, in many cultures, and even the most sceptical usually accept that pre-birth memories – and therefore pre-birth consciousness – can exist.

It is, in fact, biologically possibly to have an inkling of awareness during the final stages in the womb, though not earlier on. Soon before their birth, babies have been seen to make simple reaction movements which they will make in a more complex way after they are born – for example, the beginnings of hand grasping, or the face turning towards a touch. It's possible that the unborn baby can learn to adapt to circumstances such as noise or very bright light while in the womb, but this capacity is not seriously tested until after birth.

Based on these ideas, there has been some concern recently to treat babies with great delicacy at birth. For example, the Leboyer method of childbirth advises that the baby be born silently, in half-light, then placed on her mother's slack tummy with the cord uncut and gently stroked while they get used to one another. The idea is to provide as smooth an introduction as possible into our rough world for a birth-shocked individual. We do not know, though, whether this method of delivery has any effect on the child's emotional or intellectual development – research results so far are inconclusive.

This method assumes great awareness by the baby of what's happening to him. But nature has a way of cutting off consciousness at times when things get too much to bear. For instance, newborn babies in overstimulating conditions simply fall asleep, and most babies at birth suffer from some shortage of oxygen, which adds to their lowered awareness. What is more, the brain rhythms which would be needed for a true appreciation of what's happening aren't yet developed in the newborn. They develop slowly as the brain grows, and their absence provides a built-in protection against more mental stimulation than the baby can take. But, at very least, a quiet gentle time of birth does provide the mother with a pleasant experience which can help her to get to know her new baby more easily.

The time immediately after birth is undoubtedly very important for mothers in developing positive feelings about their babies. Many hospitals still separate mothers from their newborn babies, only allowing them to come together for feeding and changing. Mothers who are separated in this way sometimes find they are less confident about handling and mothering the baby than mothers who've had their babies close by from the beginning. Some researchers working on mother-newborn relationships believe that at the time of birth mothers develop a 'readiness' – a sort of maternal sensitivity – to become attached to their babies.[1] But this readiness needs immediate, close, physical contact in order to work properly. It is very important for mothers and their babies to be together from the time of delivery; the first three days seem to be especially important. Fathers, too, seem to be specially sensitive at their baby's birth. Those who see their babies being born feel closer to them and hold them more intimately; and this also applies to those who miss the birth, but see their babies immediately afterwards.

New parents should ask for the mother and baby to be allowed to stay together. Although the hospital staff may say that babies disturb other new mothers on the ward, every mother is in the same position and it is psychologically better for all of them to be with their babies more. It may be said that babies are kept away from mothers to reduce the risk of infection, but it sometimes seems to be more a case of administrative tidiness. If the hospital won't agree, then the simplest answer is probably for the mother to go home.

Sometimes, pain-killing drugs given to a mother during labour can make both the mother and the baby drowsy and so less responsive after birth. It is possible that this very early dulling of sensitivity can have longer term consequences in the developing mother-newborn relationship. Measurements taken of mother-baby behaviour[2] during the first year of life have shown that mothers who were drugged at the birth have to work harder to form a good relationship than those who were not. Obviously drugs have to be used at times, but they do sometimes have side-effects, so play safe and avoid them if you can. They are used in some parts of the country more than others and mothers can refuse them if they wish.

Like many relationships, that of parent with child is undoubtedly influenced by the parents' first impressions of the child. Most parents are intensely keen to see their baby 'look' at them at birth and they will try to stimulate her, if she doesn't, by stroking her face. It is part of the process of getting to know each other. Although most people assume that mothers will love their newborn babies on sight, it doesn't always happen. Love and acceptance do not appear on demand, and the baby's physical appearance and behaviour may be partly responsible for this. Certainly, some babies are easier to love than others – mothering a tiny version of your least favourite relative may not be easy.

Naturally enough, parents have expectations and fears for their unborn child – and also for themselves – before the birth. They may find themselves disappointed or even angry when the baby arrives, but it isn't always acceptable to admit to these feelings, either to themselves or to anyone else. Admitting the feelings usually makes them easier to cope with, though. For their part, babies can sense parental tension, and they react to it by crying. In this way, a particular kind of tense family lifestyle may be set up, unknowingly, right from the beginning. Even by the time they leave hospital, the mother and baby relationship can be partly moulded; so what goes on there is very important indeed.

In nearly every case any initial lack of feeling for a baby will be overcome sooner or later. Handle the baby as lovingly as possible, talk to him, give him all your attention, and slowly but surely you can expect truly loving feelings to come, and with them will grow an understanding and sensitivity which are the roots of his own feelings of well-being.

What you can do – before and at the birth
1   Try to stay calm during pregnancy.

2   Avoid poisonous drugs such as nicotine and alcohol.
3   Take care of yourself, including regular antenatal care.
4   Avoid drugs during delivery if you can.
5   Ask for a peaceful atmosphere during the baby's birth.
6   Try to keep in close contact with your baby from birth, to get to know each other.
7   If loving feelings for the baby aren't there from the start, then work towards them with as much patience as you can manage. Tell the clinic about the way you feel.
8   Talk freely with your partner about feelings for each other and the baby. A baby needs her parents to know exactly where they stand for her own emotional security.

Welcoming the newcomer

The most important part of a new baby's mental development is his social life. Obviously, physical well-being is very important indeed for a baby's survival, but all the handling, powdering and feeding that go on every day have a remarkable spin-off in developing the parents' relationship with the baby – and they can use this to help their baby develop into a competent, clever child. A mother is a baby's first courier; she is the link between the newcomer and the outside world. It's a parent's job to help the baby to take his place in society, and she starts on it from the moment he's born. Intellectual life begins at birth, and neither parent nor baby can remain unaffected by the way it progresses.

Though no-one can read a baby's mind, we can watch how she behaves with other people. It's from there that we can work out how her mental life is progressing. Here are just some of the mental facilities a brand new baby has:

Seeing   She can focus both eyes on a point about twenty centimetres away, follow a moving object with her eyes and, certainly within two weeks, distinguish colours.

Hearing   A newborn can tell differences in loudness and pitch of sound in voices, and some similar sounds like 'Pah' and 'bah'. She can be soothed by rhythmic sounds.

Smelling   This sense is well developed and newborns have strong likes (milk) and dislikes (ammonia and liquorice).

Tasting A newborn prefers sweet to salty tastes and can tell the difference between sour and bitter.

Touch Newborns are responsive to touch all over their bodies; girls may possibly be more so than boys.

Although newborn babies can't speak, they're great little communicators. From the beginning, mothers and babies are sensitive to each other's messages and start to have two-way 'conversations' with each other. At first the signals aren't very easy to see, which is probably why they've gone unrecognized in all the textbooks on child development until now. Mothers must have been aware of it all the time, but perhaps no-one thought to ask them about it. Sometimes the baby will try something out and the mother has to adjust, and sometimes it's the other way round. The 'conversations' often run in cycles. For example, one might begin with a baby looking at his mother. She responds by looking at him, and touching and talking to him. He watches and smiles back . . . then he begins to turn away . . . she tries to keep his interest . . . he closes his eyes. That is the end of that cycle. Either one of them may re-start it, and the process may take place many times without a break.

These exchanges, which take place over the first two or three months of life, indicate the style of relationship which the mother-baby couple will use together for the rest of their lives. Since each one of them is affected by messages from the other and reacts to these, each controls the other to some extent. Mothers who realize and accept that the baby has an active part to play right from the beginning will treat their baby as a person and give her the best possible start in life. This new person has her own needs, wants and intentions, which her mother learns to recognize and can translate into words for her: 'So you want a cuddle, do you?' or 'Now you're nice and cosy and ready for sleep.'

These 'conversations' are not quite democratic, though; the mother does take the lead in suggesting and demanding certain behaviour from the baby. She makes approving noises, tells him when she is pleased, and tries to discourage behaviour which she thinks is unacceptable. A sensitive mother knows when the baby is receiving her loud and clear. It's not just his behaviour that she's affecting, but his whole way of learning. It's because the mother sees her baby as a growing person that he comes, over time, to behave in something like an approved way.

Although the father's feelings about his baby aren't quite as physical – he didn't get pregnant or give birth – he normally feels very strongly attached to his baby. Unfortunately, though, a recent survey by *Woman* magazine found that the average amount of time that fathers spend alone with their babies of under a year old is less than half an hour a day. Playing and 'talking' with her father also helps the baby's mind to develop, and is very important for a balanced outlook.

The success of the communication between mothers and babies depends very much on the sensitivity and tolerance of both parties. That's why it's so difficult to judge the specific effects of a particular style of mothering. The individual nature of each baby affects his relationships and his parents' behaviour almost as powerfully as his parents affect him. No two babies respond to influences and experiences in exactly the same way, so that different styles of caring can have different effects on different babies. Parents are certainly not solely responsible for their baby's psychological world!

What you can do – for tiny babies
1 You can't spoil a newborn baby, so feel free to try; you can only do good by giving him lots of cuddling and attention.
2 Keep it very simple at this early stage and don't spend money on toys which won't interest him yet. Two or three items at a time will do.
3 Let him see different things going on by moving him around the house with you and propping him up so that he can comfortably watch the world.

4   Hang a sparkling mobile securely over his cot, from time
    to time, for him to look at. Put it about twenty centi-
    metres from his face, so that he can focus on it.

5   Paint a big face on cardboard and hang it where he can
    see it. Babies like faces and he will turn to look at it when
    he feels like it.

6   Put the baby on his tummy for at least half an hour a day
    and for five to ten minutes after meals to strengthen his
    neck muscles. If he can move his head easily, he'll see
    more.

7   Keep him with you as much as possible.

How babies organize parents

The deep love which grows between a baby and her mother
starts at birth, though it often takes months to develop fully.
Babies take a very active part in developing this love; it isn't
just a one-way process. The baby's part in forging the link
takes the form of crying, smiling, making noises – anything
that will keep her mother close. She claims more attention
for herself when she's hungry, in pain, tired or ill than when
she's well fed and comfortable. But babies vary in the way
they approach this task.

Some babies are not very good at positive feedback; they
don't give their mothers much reassurance. For example,
the baby may not appear to be delighted when he sees his
mother, yet he may show his feelings when she goes out of
sight by crying. On the other hand, some do the opposite. A
mother should watch out for the different ways her baby
uses to hold her attention and let him know, by an extra
cuddle, that his efforts are being successful; this increases his
sense of well-being and security.

But there are also babies who don't seem at all sure of
what they want – so they try out a variety of approaches to
see which is the most satisfying. This can be bewildering for
the parents, who are doing their best to make their baby
happy. Have patience and go along with your baby's
attempts to communicate, maybe even for a couple of

41

months. Together, you'll soon work out a system which is reasonably satisfactory for the whole family.

Babies in this country are usually fed on demand, which effectively means that they are taking the initiative in calling for food. Here in the West, a nursing mother may respond to her baby's cry by the oozing of a little milk from her breasts. But in South America, for example, the Mayan Indian mother starts producing milk when her baby merely moves. The Mayan mother expects to feed her baby *before* he gets hungry enough to cry; she feels for him and anticipates his wishes, rather than waiting for him to ask.

Thus, even from the time of birth, we place a hefty burden of responsibility on those tiny shoulders. Western babies are expected to make many of their own decisions about their lives; adults then respond to these, according to the way they interpret the scarcely practised instructions. Another example of this is the way the Western baby takes a hand in organizing his own comfort. He shows the way in which he would prefer to be held by complaining if it's not right and he feels uncomfortable. His mother soon gets to know his sources of comfort, as he himself learns what they are, and communication between the couple improves. By contrast, the Mayan baby has no choice, being firmly wrapped in a traditional carrying sling.

Not only does a Western baby have to demand his food and sort out his comfort, he also has to organize his sleep pattern to his own best advantage – although some babies don't seem to be very good at it. Time spent with adults is important to a baby, at the very least for food and comfort, so he has to try to be awake when people are around and asleep when they're not. After all, from the newborn's point of view, he can't be sure that there will always be someone around, and he soon learns that he's unlikely to be fed or comforted until he demands it.

Not surprisingly, the baby may suffer an unfortunate side-effect from this organizing activity, and that is anxiety. After all, if you're not sure where your next meal's coming from, right from the start, some feeling of insecurity is not unreasonable.

Some of this feeling can be seen in older children, arising from the differences between the way boys and girls are brought up. Girl babies are often allowed to be more dependent than boys. For example, their crying times may be shorter before they're seen to, and they're cuddled more than boys without having to ask for it first. What happens then is that the older boys get, the less easy they find it to ask for help from others; they are supposed to be more independent than girls. This can be seen also in grown men, who have a greater fear of dependency than women do.

Often unknowingly, parents encourage signs of independence in babies of both sexes from the time they are born. Little signs of independence are usually watched for, and approved of warmly – like a baby pushing away the bottle when she's had enough. I once heard a mother, speaking for her baby's independence, say: 'We had to leave the maternity ward early as Roger [the baby] had had enough, and wanted to go home.'

The more freedom we give our babies to organize their own lives, the more kindness and security they need. Love and kindness are not the same thing, and babies need kindness too.

What you can do – to cooperate with your baby
1   Watch out for any signs she gives you such as a glance, a cry or a hand movement and react to them promptly with an extra cuddle to show you've got the message.
2   Try to keep in tune with your baby. If you know what's on her mind, you can think ahead of her and anticipate her wishes. That way she can relax in the confidence that she will be provided for.
3   Make sure that babies get lots of loving contact; in particular, give a boy as much as you would to a girl.
4   Be kind, as well as loving, to your baby.

Can you tell if a newborn baby is clever?

Clever babies are probably more alert when they're born than other babies. Some can hold their heads up alone, for a moment or two, right from the start, and seem to be looking around and taking life in with great interest. Sometimes, doctors and nurses will tell parents if a baby seems to be more alert than is usual, but then . . . they may say that to all mums.

Babies who are particularly sensitive and responsive are often clever too. You can feel this responsiveness when you hold the baby. For example, if a baby seems to back away from something it shows that she can distinguish between what's pleasant for her and what's not – and that's the beginning of mental activity. More sensitive babies are more easily tickled too.

The earlier you see your baby smile, the more likely she is to be clever. Though this isn't a totally reliable sign of cleverness, it's an indication, and very early smilers often turn out to be clever children.

Very intelligent children were often bigger and heavier at birth, though not always. The reason for this is that big, healthy babies are more likely to be born to mothers who have been well nourished and cared for in their pregnancies. It's those same mothers who are more likely to give their children the best educational help at home, which will show up later on intelligence tests. It's possible, too, that heavier babies have a psychological advantage as well as a better physcial start in life, because they have reason to be more contented than other babies. They can take in more food at once, for example, so they need less frequent feeding and can turn their energies in more intellectual directions. In addition, their parents, relieved of the constant preoccupation with feeding and cleaning that smaller babies need, may feel that such a baby is more of a social person and so behave differently towards him. So, even from birth, heavier and more attractive babies probably find themselves in a more pleasant and emotionally supportive world than lighter ones,

44

and benefit from this initial good fortune in many ways throughout life.

Different abilities in newborns develop at different rates and, though there's some co-ordination between them, it would never do to measure the growth of one or two abilities and judge how the rest were likely to come on from these. Some of a baby's skills are related to her degree of physical development, others to experience, and some to both. In trying to judge very early signs of cleverness, always look at your baby as a whole person. In general, you could say that clever babies show all-round advancement in their development, and the likelihood is that, with their parents' help, they will keep that advantage.

What a clever baby needs

The most important psychological benefit which parents can give their new baby is super-generous amounts of loving physical cuddling. This means holding the baby in an upright position a lot, and having plenty of eye contact. It gives the baby the reassurance he needs to build up his feeling of security, which in turn builds the base for exploration and learning, and later for self-reliance. You can't 'spoil' tiny babies by cuddling them too much.

Research on newborn babies in Zambia by the American Professor Brazelton[3] found that by the time the babies were five days old they were already more advanced than American babies and that they were even more so by ten days old. They kept this lead until they were about two years old, when the American babies studied began to overtake them on simple tests of mental ability. He thought that this very early advance was due to the way the babies were handled. The tribal mother of Zambia carries her baby around in a cloth sling, usually on her back. The baby is fed when he cries, sleeps with his mother and is handled quite roughly by Western standards. For example, a Zambian mother positions the baby on her back by gripping one of his elbows under her armpit and swinging him over her shoulder. The later slowing up of his progress is probably due to the arrival of another baby, when he is pushed aside, loses his supply of mother's milk and goes on to a nutritionally poor diet.

It's the close physical contact between mothers and babies which makes it very much easier for them to get to know one another. When the mother is holding the baby close and looking at him, she's in a much better position to make immediate responses to his signals. The quicker her response, the more likely the baby is to retain his new learning (very early learning is easily forgotten). Tiny babies aren't much good at remembering what's happened before, so a mother may have to respond to the same signals over and over again, and this is easier for them both if she's close by at the right times.

Babies have a real need to build up a relationship at this very early age. They are satisfied with one good one, though they can cope with more. They need the opportunity to explore their world within this relationship, most particularly by means of their 'conversations' with another person. This is where the foundations of understanding and language are laid. The baby's activities are not simply directed towards making life more comfortable, though – they are a positive attempt to make life more lively, in a sense, to stir things up, so he can learn from his own sensitivities and vulnerabilities. Babies are born predisposed to social life which enables them, in time, to develop into social people. The newborn human baby needs love (physical and emotional), adult responsiveness, stimulation and total acceptance.

Isn't she clever!

The human mind is active right from the start. Soon after birth, a baby begins to select and organize her experiences. All the time, when she's awake, she is reacting to what's going on around her and doing her best to cope with the information she gathers. Sights and sounds don't just flow over her in a haphazard way, they are attended to systematically; some are dismissed and some are stored in the beginnings of memory for later. Right from the start the baby is striving to learn, trying out different ways of doing things, experimenting all the time and judging the value of the results. Although she is barely aware in the adult sense of what she is doing, the world is a very complicated business to sort out, and she gets on with it right away.

Mental development is not something which parents can impose from the outside, nor is it merely a matter of sitting back and allowing natural abilities to unfold like a flower bud. It's an active process, in which the baby has a big part to play. The baby searches out her own learning, so that she never depends entirely on what chance may bring for her mental stimulation – she makes things happen by cooing or crying to catch attention. If a baby were only to lie back passively and wait for experience, very little might happen; she certainly wouldn't be able to practise communication, which she so clearly does do, at the start of life.

When a baby is born she has some unthinking physical reflexes, and these shouldn't be confused with mental activity. She can, for example, grasp an adult finger if it's forced into her little fist. If she's held in the right position, she can make walking movements; and when laid flat on her face, she can raise her head. But though these reflexes are useful, the newborn hasn't any actual skills; they still have to be learnt.

Video recording has provided a big breakthrough in understanding very tiny babies. Their behaviour is often so fleeting that much of what we can see now, in close-up and in slow motion, could never have been seen before. The video tapes can be run through over and over again, until every detail of the scene is familiar to the viewer, and sometimes subtle movements may only be spotted after several replays.

A double-screen technique has been devised that splits the pictures of a mother with her baby so they can be shown on two separate screens at the same time. This method can provide a view of the behaviour of each one of them when they are together, which is easier for comparison than having them in the same frame. Because it's only in the last few years that these techniques have been used, even fairly recent textbooks on child development haven't been able to report the findings and many details are still to be found only in research documents. Here are just some of the discoveries:

Eye contact

The baby's inborn capacity for eye-to-eye contact provides the key factor in forging the link between mother and baby. From birth, babies seem to be fascinated by the human face and can recognize their mother's face within a week. By one month old, a baby can take in enough information about faces to sort out familiar from unfamiliar ones. All newborn babies are short-sighted, but mothers usually hold their faces naturally at the right distance from their babies' – that is, less than thirty centimetres away.

Watching

From birth, a baby can follow a large object with his eyes for a few seconds if it's held at the right distance, though he can't manage smaller ones yet. Within a week he'll move his eyes purposely about and will soon become selective in what he looks at, such as following his own hand movements. Just a few days after birth, almost all babies can follow a red light, moving their heads and eyes to do this. During this action, they focus all their behaviour on the task of co-ordinating vision, body movement and attention.

Listening

Within seconds of birth, babies can detect the direction of a sound, and turn their face towards it. At only 12 hours old, they can spot the diffeence between human speech and other sounds, reacting with barely visible rhythmic movements which show up on a slow-motion video recording. Mother and baby learn about each other by using sound, by 'talking' and 'listening' to each other. A baby shouldn't be left alone for long periods of time with no-one around to talk or listen. This is because she needs to be able to practise the constant wordless 'chatter' with other people that forms this very early foundation of her future language.

Sensitivity

Babies are born with all five senses working. Although no two babies are alike in their alertness and in the speed of their responses, all are very sensitive to changes in what's going on around them. A newborn will startle or cry at what seems to an adult like only a barely noticeable change in the surroundings, such as a new voice speaking. A baby will close his eyes or turn his head away from a light that's too bright or a movement which is too disturbing for him.

A mother should watch out to see that her baby is not overloaded with messages. What happens then is that the baby will probably 'switch off', so that she offers shorter and shorter spans of attention and can miss out on aspects of this very early learning. The mother's sensitivity must be the guide; keep looking at your baby to see whether she turns away from your attentions. If she does, then cut down for a while on trying to make her react.

Smiling

Mothers have often said that their babies could smile by the end of the second week, to which doctors and nurses have replied that it's only wind. Now, thanks to video, we have much evidence to show that mothers are right. These very early smiles are in fact the products of highly organized behaviour, which shows the beginnings of thought. They're different from later smiles, though, as they arise from feelings that the baby has inside, rather than as responses to others' smiles. The first few may be a reaction to the mother's voice, or they may be due to a change in the baby's surroundings. Too great a change, though, may only produce tension and crying; too little, and the baby will ignore it. In a couple of months, as the baby gets more sophisticated, these spontaneous smiles are increasingly replaced by genuine social smiles.

Copying

The new video techniques have shown that, contrary to

previous opinion, babies can imitate their mothers' facial and body movements to some extent soon after birth. A fourteen-day-old baby can even imitate a finger movement in an adult sitting next to him. Babies begin to imitate patterns of speech movement with their lips from a few weeks old, but they are able to distinguish between some different speech sounds even from birth. Speech begins here. Talk to your baby as much as you like; he'll understand your tone even if the words are beyond him, and he will like the rhythm.

Crying

Crying is the main means of early voice communication which the baby uses to bring someone near her. There are a variety of cries, with different strengths and rhythms, which send different messages. Parents know the difference between a cry of hunger and one of fear. Don't let a baby 'cry it out' too often, as it restricts her communication skills. Give her a regular, prompt response to cries when you can, as this is more likely to bring about a better quality of relationship between you and her and so cut down on the crying. When the baby learns that her cries are likely to be answered immediately, she'll be more inclined to branch out and try other, more subtle forms of getting your attention as well, and she will also be less intense in her demands.

Answering a tiny baby's cry doesn't lead to a 'spoilt' child, as is sometimes thought, though some babies are more easily soothed than others. An 'easy' baby will respond readily to a wide variety of calming efforts on the part of his parents, such as being rocked, stroked or shifted from a flat to an upright position. Some say that girl babies are more 'soothable'. A fussy baby may not respond very much to normal soothing, so that her mother may feel less adequate as a mother. A baby's 'soothability' dictates the kind of care that she receives – the more easily soothed a baby is, the more attention she gets. The best way to stop a baby crying is to hold her up on your shoulder. This usually makes her open her eyes and look around. If your baby is one of those who aren't very cuddly, try raising up her baby-seat instead, by putting it on a table for example.

But whatever you do, it's a fact that some babies cry more than others, and parents have to judge for themselves how best to cope with their baby's crying. If it's getting on top of you and she doesn't seem to be responding to your attentions, don't hesitate to seek help.

Premature birth

Being born before time isn't usually considered to give a baby the best start in life, though eight per cent of babies begin that way. But some very recently discovered facts allow us to understand how the effects of prematurity and low birth weight can be overcome. Judging babies' mental ability poses a problem – should it be made by age, or by level of physical maturity? Overall, the baby's age after birth is usually the better measure, but the development of some abilities depends on physical maturity. Brain waves, for example, develop in accordance with age, so a premature baby is likely to have a similar brain wave pattern and be as mentally developed as a full-term baby of the same age. But, on the other hand, the way the baby's vision develops is tied to his rate of physical growth, which is slower in a premature baby.

Unfortunately, premature babies often have to cope with extra disadvantages in addition to their early birth; they usually have to undergo more stress than other babies. A premature baby incubator, though vital for life, isn't the ideal place for encouraging mental development. In the hospital unit, light and sound go on twenty-four hours a day; this is an abnormal situation which can affect the baby's delicate mental and muscle co-ordination. Being in conditions like these could have bad effects on an adult too. But the main problem for an incubator baby is the lack of normal experiences to learn from, together with the overload of disorganized, confusing experiences of sights and sounds, which can go on for weeks. Where it's possible to offer these

51

babies a more normal environment, it can be seen to make a big improvement in their overall development. For example, babies who have been taken from their incubators regularly for cuddling, or who lie on softer bedding, or have rhythmic sounds played to them, gain weight faster, are mentally more responsive, and are better co-ordinated than those who do not have these experiences.

These hiccups in a premature baby's development call for extra attention when she comes home, so that she can catch up with anything she may have missed out on. For example, because the baby's vision isn't as well developed as a full-term baby's, the mother will find that she has to make a special effort to build up her relationship with the baby. Eye-to-eye contact is the basis of learning and the intellectual development of the newborn's mind, but mothers may find this more difficult if the baby is premature. It's essential for the mother to put a lot into building up this relationship – it won't be as much of a two-way partnership as it will be later, but it is a beginning.

Because of these less rewarding visual responses, as well as the baby's limited ability to pay attention (due to immaturity), parents of premature babies need to take special care to see that the baby gets his full share of experiences once he's at home. Some researchers, though, have described a 'catch up' phenomenon built into children's development. In rural Guatemala, newborn infants are kept in a darkened room and they are allowed very little stimulation during the first year of their lives. This is meant to protect them. When measured for mental development, they were found to be retarded at the ages of two to three years old[3], but they caught up, more or less, in later childhood. This phenomenon probably applies as well to children who are hospitalized or ill-nourished for some time after birth.

All babies are physically at their most vulnerable at birth and in the first few weeks of life, which is why medical advice must normally predominate at this time. Parents whose babies are in special medical care sometimes feel that their own natural feelings about wanting to hold them should be kept under control, except at permitted times like feeding. But it's very important for the psychological growth of all babies, however physically fragile, that they should begin to make physical contact and build up relationships from birth. It may be necessary in some hospitals to insist on at least stroking your baby, and you can always talk to her, but doctors and nurses are usually ready to fit in with parents' wishes for the baby's benefit, so there may not be a problem.

In these first few weeks of life, parents' most trustworthy guide to coping is their own sensitivity to the baby's searching and exploring activities. Part of that sensitivity lies in knowing what the baby is capable of doing, and part of it is in helping her to practise her brand new learning.

What you can do – for the baby's mind
From birth

1 Remember that the baby is aware from the start, so encourage him to develop a taste for exploration, e.g. by holding your face and bright objects fairly close to his eyes. He can then see and touch with his fingers, so that he also learns from feeling.
2 Be sensitive to what interests him, such as your hair or a strange noise, and encourage his involvement with these things.
3 Put a stainless steel mirror (firmly secured) over his cot, about twenty centimetres from his face, so that he can see his reflection. He'll have a lot of fun pulling faces at himself. Attach it to a semi-rigid structure, such as a length of plastic, for him to reach up for when he's able to. Dangling things are hard to grasp.
4 Don't put a great number of objects in or around the cot; too much 'enrichment' only turns him off.
5 Listen to his cries and coos, and react to them promptly.
6 Make a 'cradle-gym' of toys he can reach, strung across his cot or pram, so that he can knock them, watch them swing and learn some hand-to-eye coordination.

From six months

1   Give him just a few tough toys that won't fall to pieces when bitten or thrown. They should not be too small – say, less than five centimetres in diameter – or he may swallow them.

2   Try a kick toy tied to the foot end of the cot. A large flat piece of foam rubber covered in vinyl, showing a big toy face and little body and tied on with strong elastic, will give hours of pleasure and leg exercise.

3   Talk about what you're doing, such as putting on socks, all the time. Repeat key words over and over.

4   Give the baby free time on a blanket on the floor every day. He'll begin to crawl and explore more quickly.

5   Let him handle things that work, like switching the light on, and when he succeeds, say 'light'. Babies also love a jack-in-the-box.

6   Make safe areas for him to explore when he begins to crawl. Freedom to explore is very important.

7   Always respond to a baby. If, for example, you are on the telephone, break off and tell the child 'Wait a minute'. It's better than ignoring him.

8   Play involving games like hide-and-seek.

9   Use playpens or any other restraining devices like high chairs only as long as the baby looks contented in them. When he shows signs of boredom, take him out.

10 Keep life lively for the baby by changing his scenery, talking to him and interesting him in your daily activities. No-one is more interesting to a baby than his mother. Exaggerate your own actions slightly to make them clearer, such as speaking slowly and making clear facial expressions and body movements.

Chapter 3

THE MAKING OF MINDS

Mind and body have such a very close working relationship that one hardly ever acts without the other – they both co-operate with and affect each other all the time. Thought and emotions from the mind are needed for body movements to take place (except for automatic reflexes). For example, the brain area which deals with leg movements needs the cooperation of the mind in the wish to move. For that matter, breaking a leg can make you feel depressed.

Whenever we humans use our minds and bodies, we do it according to the way we've learned, since birth, to fit in and cope with the world. The human mind has a natural tendency to put some order into what's going on around it. We enjoy sorting and classifying and making rules about life – listen to any toddler as she discovers these joys. Many of the rules we make up don't seem to have any real purpose, or to make sense, but are just a sort of intellectual exercise. We like to make forbidding rules too; a group of children making up a game can sort out a hundred 'dos' and 'don'ts' in no time. But the negative rules often have an emotional basis in fear, such as 'Don't walk under a ladder' or 'Don't walk on the cracks in the pavement'.

After a century's investigation into the nature of intelli-gence, people may be forgiven for thinking that psychologists still don't know their own minds. But there *is* such a thing as intelligence – it's not a myth and it need not be a mystery either. The problem is that intelligence cannot be measured as a clear-cut mental power in the same way that, say, physical power can be measured by the weight of dumb-bells lifted. There are so many aspects to intelligence that tests can only measure parts of it and we're not sure how they overlap. Perhaps it is easiest to think of intelligence as a

55

shapeless moving collection of different thinking abilities such as reasoning, critical judgement, flexibility of mind and original thinking, which all work together. Different statistical methods have produced over a hundred different kinds of thinking abilities, though the margin between them is sometimes too small to be seen by the 'naked eye'.

The talkers

One of the earliest forms of language, both for the human race and for each baby, is giving a name to things. Even now, naming has some magical qualities which our more primitive ancestors would have recognized. Some religions, for example, refuse to name their god for fear of what might happen. The 'doing' words usually come next, and then words for more abstract ideas. Children have to learn the sounds and meanings of whatever language is spoken by their parents, and they also acquire the thought processes which have developed in that language over the centuries of its use. In this way, children's thoughts and behaviour and use of language are inextricably bound up together. For example, a child's simple demand, 'Pick me up', tells us a lot about her mental activity – for instance, that she sees herself as distinct from other people, believes in her own power of command, and that she associates the physical act of being lifted with particular emotional needs and responses.

The way we use words gives a good indication of the way our minds work. Thought has to be put into words so that it can be communicated; and for it to be put into words, it first has to be sorted into categories. We think; then we want to say what we think, and express it somehow – so new words are born, while others fade from lack of use. Pre-1960 no-one would have understood 'laid-back' or 'swinging' in the way we use them today. And we, of course, don't understand all those archaic words which television quiz shows like 'Call My Bluff' dig up as teasers; their usefulness as conveyors of ideas has long since passed away. We don't talk today about 'loafers', 'swells', or 'bounders'. Language which is alive is always open to change, and we who speak it are changing it all the time.

Learning to talk is probably the single most important part of a child's intellectual development. It begins right from birth (as described in Chapter 2) with the 'conversations' between mothers and their babies. Parents who are generous in listening and responding to their babies are starting them firmly on the right path to good language development. The better this kind of intellectual parenting has been, the greater the baby's intellectual development. Fortunately, babies have an inborn grasp of language which makes it easy for them to learn quickly. By four years old, children are so proficient in their language that they can help younger ones learn to speak, and even simplify their language so that it can be better understood.

To help a baby's language ability develop, it's essential for parents to spend as much time as they can in conversation with him. The baby's babbling or first stumbling efforts to talk should be listened to very carefully and then answered, as far as possible, in a way that the baby is able to take in. To do this, it's important to speak directly to an infant, at eye-to-eye level, whenever you can. But babies still go on learning, even when you aren't talking to them.

A child can only improve her talking when she's ready for it; you can't force-feed language, because the baby just won't accept it. For example, a baby of two months old can imitate and learn to use vowel sounds, but she can't manage consonants yet. She'll begin to pick them up in another couple of months, though. The baby's first year of language learning holds a number of keys to her later talking and thinking abilities. For example, her early babblings contain all the sounds she is going to use as a child. They can even give an idea of how intelligent the child is going to be. Heavy babblers often grow up to be clever children. On the other hand, it can be disappointing that babies who can speak before they're expected to don't necessarily grow up to be more articulate or clever, because very early speech is more like imitation than considered utterances.

The most striking and probably most effective difference between the experience of clever and less clever children is in the amount of conversation their families make, both with the baby and with each other. Not only the amount, of course, but the quality is important too. It's in the family setting that a child learns to use language to express his ideas, and in using it, develops a style of intellectual activity.

Much of what we understand through our senses – especially hearing and seeing – comes about because of the way we were brought up to use language. When there isn't much talk in a home, thoughts and ideas stand much less of a chance to be practised and to develop. But this does not automatically result in early speech. Many famous people, Winston Churchill being the best known example, haven't started to speak until they were well into childhood. But his late speech gave no indication of Churchill's later brilliant spoken and written English.

It can help you to get a true picture of your baby's talking if you keep a simple record of what she can say. She may start out by sounding some consonants like 'r' and 'p' from around six months, and from then till she's about a year old, her babbling usually goes on at a great rate. A baby is likely to have a few words in hand by the time she's a year old, though not necessarily, and then she moves swiftly on.

Babies begin by giving names to what they see around them every day – usually moveable things. They often start with food and drink, then go on to animals, clothes and toys. Nowadays, a baby is more likely to say 'car' before 'house'. At fourteen to twenty months, mothers still need to name things for the child; if she says 'doll' in an expectant voice, the baby will try to repeat it. But she should keep the pressure on – as soon as he seems to master that one, she can then test him, asking 'What is it?'. Her expectations should be just a little ahead of what he's managed to do so far.

Between eighteen months and two years old, babies start to put words together like 'Daddy go car'. It's the beginning of grammar, but they've still got a way to go. Then, as the child's talking develops, she begins to move away from the here-and-now, so that she can begin to tell her listener something, and ask simple questions. Parents can help by asking her: 'What did you do? What did you see?'

Each group of people, even one as small as a family, has its own rules about language; the child has to learn to fit in with the rules of this game. He starts by learning the general way people around him speak and think, then tightens up on the rules as he is corrected. For example, an adult might say, 'Would you be so kind as to post this letter?' But the speaker is not really asking the listener to outline his degree of kindness. What appears grammatically to be a question is really a demand – wrapped up in convention – and this is the way language is actually used. A child's sensitivity to the way adults think helps him to learn the rules of language; this goes for the later learning of foreign languages too.

When they make mistakes in speaking, children are still going by rules, even though their rules may be wrong. By five years old, children can learn the right rules so well that they can speak with hardly a mistake. But the more practice and attention children have in language learning, the better they will be at it.

In everyday conversations, even with very tiny children, parents can use language to help enlarge a child's ideas about the topic of the moment. A simple example might go as follows. *Jimmy* (aged 3): 'I'm going to be fireman when I grow up.' *Mother:* 'A fireman hmm. So you can put out lots of fires with great big hoses.' *Jimmy:* 'I'll splash water everywhere.' *Mother:* 'Then you might not have enough left to put out the fire with.' *Jimmy:* 'Well, I'll put most of it on the fire.'

If Jimmy's original idea hadn't been taken up at this point, he probably wouldn't have gone on to consider how much water it would take to put the fire out. This exchange, though tiny, has notched another peg of Jimmy's understanding. But even information conversation is an art; if Jimmy's mother had begun to list aspects of fire-fighting in an attempt to teach him too much, the likelihood is that he would have switched off and learned very little.

To have the greatest learning effect, topics of conversation must be interesting to the child and should only go on for as long as she shows interest. You can tell what a little baby is interested in by seeing how long she looks at something. Then you can talk about it to her, even before she can speak – babies can understand meaning long before they can talk. As children get older, their conversations get longer and more complicated, but they will let you know when they've had enough of a topic. Intelligent listening will always be one of the most important presents that parents can give a clever child. Children don't learn to speak by parrot-like imitation; they learn in pleasurable social situations, where they can practise all they already know, and go on to try a bit more. Showing pleasure at your baby's efforts to make sounds gives her the encouragement to go on learning.

Talking to a baby is not just a watered-down version of talking to an adult. You're not only communicating, you're also teaching, all the time. The more the baby's language improves, the more scope he has for learning more. Language can be self-generating.

Here are a few hints for speaking to babies or little children:
* Repeat what you say.
* Keep to the here-and-now.
* Speak quite loudly.
* Be clear in your pronunciation.
* Ask simple questions.

Questions
As they get older children begin to ask questions, but clever children ask different kinds of questions from less clever ones. Where ordinary children will ask more 'what?' questions, like 'What's that thing called?' or 'Where is my teddy?', the clever child asks more 'Why?' questions, such as 'Why is the moon in the sky?'. These 'why' questions are often more difficult to answer, sometimes even impossible,

60

but they come from a searching, growing intelligence and shouldn't be answered in a patronizing or offhand way.

Parents should try to answer 'why' questions in as impersonal a way as the child can accept at her age. This helps her to think outwards from her own tiny world into a more abstract way of thinking and reasoning. Unfortunately, parents who feel unsure about their own ability to answer these (sometimes deep-sounding) questions often try to avoid answering them factually, even though the child's own understanding is very limited and she needs information. Here is an example. *Mother:* 'It's four o'clock.' *Annie* (aged 3): 'Why is it four o'clock?' *Mother:* 'Because your tea's ready.' *Annie:* Silence.

A better response would have been for Annie's mother to say: 'Well, when we had dinner, it was one o'clock; then we went shopping so the clock went one, two, three, and now it's four o'clock, and time for tea.' *Annie:* 'I like four o'clock.'

Children are constantly on the look-out, trying to understand what's going on. When they come to events and remarks which don't make sense to them, they should feel free to ask about them. They are always working towards building up a picture of what they see, but they suspect they might not have it right, so they are always vulnerable to a 'put-down'. Children's questions are almost always serious (though they sometimes get out of hand when the children find that it's a good way of getting extra attention).

A problem with children's questions is that they can't always express themselves very clearly, and may ask questions which are misleading, especially if parents aren't listening very carefully. Children can believe, for example, that television characters are real, or they may not understand adult social customs, like paying a bill. 'Is Bill a window cleaner? Do you only pay one Bill? Are all window cleaners called Bill? Why doesn't Bill pay you?' Their questions may be perfectly logical – within the limits of their knowledge. What may appear to be ridiculous questioning may not be childish or attention-seeking, but the efforts of a clever child who has worked something out (if incorrectly) and who wants to know more.

Children need time to work through their own thoughts, and it helps to encourage this intellectual curiosity. An only child gets much more opportunity to do this than a child with brothers and sisters. Parents and children also need to have built up a certain trust for the child to feel able to try out strange paths of thought. This comes about through plenty of shared experience. Spending their days together helps parents to understand their child; long periods of separation make it much more difficult.

But children have a great sense of humour too, which anxious adults can miss. I once heard a clever five-year-old girl ask: 'What's the difference between a dinosaur's bone and a chicken bone?' The serious adults present considered various educated answers. Was it evolutionary, or the difference between birds and reptiles? They all gave different answers. 'Wrong,' she said. 'One's smaller.'

What you can do – language
For babies

1 Keep physically close to a baby; 'talk' and 'listen' as much as you can.

2 Offer your baby simple things like a toy and a comb, and see which he looks at. Then pick this object up and show it to him; 'talk' about it together. Show him other things in the house in the same way, like a dripping tap.

3 When your baby is about a year old, teach him to point to things and name them.

4 Recite nursery rhymes for rhythm and pleasure.

5 Read to him and show him the pictures in books, from the time he is a few months' old.

6 See if the few words your baby knows have anything in common – shape, colour or texture. Show him similar things, and talk about what's the same and what's different.

7   Keep using the same words and phrases, so that your baby gets to know the sound of them.

8   Encourage the baby to take the lead in conversation, and to take pleasure in it.

For toddlers

1   Praise effort, and don't correct grammar too often.

2   Keep 'baby talk' to a minimum.

3   Use the same 'key' words over and over again.

4   Describe things which are physically present, so that he can coordinate all that he can hear, see and touch.

5   Keep your conversation as lively and interesting to the child as possible.

6   Help the child use the words he already knows.

7   Answer properly, not just by saying 'Oh' – it's conversation you're after.

Brain and mind

Both the physical make-up of the brain and the way it operates affect a person's intelligence. For a detailed look at how it works as well as an idea of how it develops, see a book such as *Human Biology* by Joan Freeman[1].

For our purposes here, the brain can be thought of as a highly complicated switchboard in a telephone system, though one big difference is that thought messages are transmitted almost immediately. It operates by using special body cells – nerve cells – called neurones, which are densely packed in the brain. Each nerve cell stores images, which are taken in and sent on to other neurones by an electric current that jumps across a tiny gap (synapse) between neurones.

Thinking is the result of up to ten billion neurones constantly exchanging information. It is thought that a single neurone can connect with as many as a thousand other neurones at the same time. The more information-passing fibres a neurone can develop, the greater its ability to transmit information. In theory, there is no limit to the amount of material the brain can cope with. On that basis, if we could increase the branching of the information-giving fibres, we could improve intelligence. One theory is that very intelligent people have more of these branching fibres than less intelligent people, which would explain how they can process information so much more efficiently. Another is that the more a child uses a particular nerve route, the quicker the synapse gap is jumped, in which case mental exercises such as mental arithmetic or lively discussion should be beneficial.

Psychological research on rats has shown that the thicker the fatty coating around each nerve fibre, the quicker they conduct information and the more intelligently the rats behave. This thickness was found to increase when the rats were handled more by their keepers and also when they were given a more stimulating task – in the rats' case this took the form of a more complicated maze to negotiate. It is quite possible that human information-processing is similarly affected. So, if we transfer these findings to children, it would follow that intelligence – or at least speed of thought – could be nurtured through physical affection and a stimulating learning environment.

The brain is something of a computer, too, as it seems to operate mostly on programmes. The information which the nerve cells store can either be in individual bits or in chains. A simple body action, such as raising a little finger, simultaneously triggers off millions of circuits – exactly the right ones for the job. Whatever we learn is stored in programmes for further use, but as we are human beings and not computers our brains tend to use these programmes in an emotional way. For example, we are not keen to take in new learning unless it seems interesting or rewarding. In other words, we learn best what we want to learn.

Clever children can cope with more complicated programmes than average children and can use their better storage facilities – memory – and their often better concentration to develop new ideas. Parents can encourage their children to develop this storage capacity by being positive and giving praise for good memory instead of offering the more usual put-down remarks for forgetfulness, such as 'You'd forget your head if it wasn't screwed on!' You could also use memory improvement games, such as this variation of Kim's game. To play, put a selection of small objects such as a rubber band, doll's shoe, a toy teacup and a little box on a tray; then cover it with a cloth. Do this without the children watching. Then show the covered tray to the children, take the cloth off for five seconds, cover it again and get the children to draw what they remember of it. Count up how many things they've remembered, and give a score too for whether they've put them in the right positions as well as for how well they've drawn them. It's fun, as well as being an excellent learning-to-learn game.

The way the brain works is also influenced by hormones. These are body chemicals, made by the glands, which affect our body functions, especially our emotions. For example, if a child has a negative attitude to what he's supposed to be learning, or is bored, frightened or tired, the thymus gland gives off hormones (endorphins) which can actually block new information getting to the highest levels of brain processing. 'Exam nerves' are an example of the action of fear and hormones. You may have faced an exam paper and found that you couldn't remember a thing, and though you struggled valiantly to put something down, even answers which you knew perfectly the day before seemed to have vanished. One way of overcoming this problem in children's learning is to try to keep it interesting and tension-free, and give lots of praise so they feel good about it. Don't try to cram material into tired children. Children are not empty vessels waiting to be filled, they are eager learners ready for the revelation that you will provide.

Right brain and left brain
For centuries, great thinkers have written about the split between thinking based on reason and emotion. But it is only since the late 1950s that psychologists, particularly Robert Ornstein[2] in America, have discovered that this differentiation is due to the different influences of the two physical

65

halves of the brain. It began with observing epileptics and patients who'd had brain injuries where either the two halves of the brain had become separated or there was damage to specific parts of the brain.

People who are dominated in their thinking by the right half of their brain tend to see things as a whole. They are concerned with patterns, shapes and sizes, and are more imaginative and intuitive. Their ideas can seem vague and woolly to left-brain dominated people who are often better at more logical and academic work such as mathematics and word skills. Whereas the right side will help you to hum a tune, write a poem or see a painting as a whole, the left side will help you to write grammatically, mend an engine or admire the brush technique of the artist. But for most people the two halves work together in harmony, so that the brain is not so much one computer, but two, working together for better effect.

It seems that the seeds of knowledge are largely absorbed in gulps by the more spontaneous right brain, and then they are sorted out and communicated by the left brain. Each half can do the other's work to some extent but functions better when the incoming information fits its style of processing. But it isn't always the appropriate half which tackles incoming information. Most people have a bias to one side which gives them their special style, but which can interfere with aspects of their learning. For example, poor spellers may be biased to use their right brain more than their left, so they rely too much on their intuition and don't pay enough attention to the details of the letters.

Babies and toddlers don't usually have a dominant half to their brain, but traditional teaching in schools has emphasized left-brain activity sometimes to the detriment of the right, so that the left brain is usually the more dominant by the time children leave school. School and IQ tests, for example, are designed more for the left brain than the right. Some psychologists even believe that if certain right-brain activities are not exercised regularly they will never develop properly and that, as the greatest creative achievements require both halves of the brain, an overly academic education cuts down a child's creative potential. Lately, teachers have begun to cultivate the more intuitive, creative right brain. Here are a couple of short lists of the ways in which children who are dominated by one side or the other are likely to behave:

Left brain	Right brain
Likes formal teaching	Likes low lights and warmth
Is persistent	Not keen to sit and learn
Is responsible	Likes learning in company
Is happy learning alone	Likes moving around, touching and doing things
Stays still while learning	
Does well at school	Doesn't do brilliantly at school

It is possible that there are sex differences in right- and left-brain use. Girls are usually said to be dominated by the right brain, being intuitive; boys are said to be left-brain dominated, better at mathematics and engineering. But as babies do not show any signs of this specialization, which increases as children get older, it is very likely that it is the way each sex is brought up which influences their style of thinking. Any child can get into lopsided thinking habits, starting from about four years old. Parents can watch out for this and try to correct the balance to help the child become mentally agile.

Another way of looking at this division of thinking styles is to group children as divergent or convergent thinkers. This corresponds pretty well with right- and left-brain thinkers respectively. A convergent thinker goes by the rules, will probably reach conclusions quite logically and generally does well in scientific, mathematical activities. Divergent thinkers are more creative, coming up with new and maybe crazy-sounding ideas and approaches, and often lean towards artistic activities. Convergent-minded children do better with straightforward question-and-answer-type tests, and divergent people prefer essays where they can use their imagination.

A typical test of convergent/divergent thinking is to ask a child what uses can be made of a brick. *The converger* builds houses, builds walls, props up shelves etc. *The diverger* uses it as a paperweight, crumbles it to make cement, throws it through a window etc.

It is sometimes said that to encourage divergent thinking is only to encourage a child to be silly – which says something about the people who say this. It's not that a child is completely one or the other kind of thinker – we need to be both to survive – but it's the dominant style we're interested in here.

What you can do – thinking

1   Give lots of physical affection – touching and hugging – so that the child feels wanted and valued. Children who feel good in themselves learn better and think more.

2   Keep plenty of material around for the child to learn from and with.

3   Encourage keenness, concentration and memory by showing delight in them.

4   Show the child your own enthusiasm for ideas.

5   Keep the child's learning as exciting as you can, or at least interesting. Boredom is a great turn-off.

6   Don't try to push new information into a tired child. It's not your perseverance that counts, it's the child's own desire to carry on that matters.

7   Try to keep the tension level in your home as low as you can. It can act as a block on a growing mind.

8   Dance together to music on the radio to loosen up physically before you settle down to a quiet thinking and talking time.

9   Lower the lighting sometimes and play different kinds of music while you talk together about ideas and matters that concern you both. Listen carefully to your child's words before you answer.

10 If you feel your child is right-brain dominated, encourage the left side by playing games such as the puzzles you see in children's comics – find Farmer MacDonald's pig, for instance, hidden in a drawing of his farmyard.

11 If your child seems to be left-brain dominated, encourage an appreciation of big things like the way the sky meets the earth, or give out great big pieces of paper to paint on with a big brush.

What about IQ?

Although the term IQ is used quite freely by parents, teachers and psychologists, considerable controversy rages as to what it really is. Earlier this century, it was thought that intelligence was fixed for life at the time of conception. But now we know that it varies a lot with circumstances, and can even change from day to day. Not only can each individual's score vary, but different tests produce different IQs. For instance, of the two most frequently used intelligence tests, one has an upper limit of IQ 145 and the other of IQ 170. The same child measured on the two tests can come out with an average of seven IQ points difference in score. Sometimes, tests which are designed to measure specific skills, like reading, are mistakenly used to judge IQ (I have seen this happen).

The letters 'IQ' stand for Intelligence Quotient – the quotient being the result of an arithmetical division. It is a number calculated from the score a child reaches in an intelligence test. This score is called her mental age, and it is divided by her chronological age, then multipled by a hundred to round it off, thus:

$$\frac{\text{Mental age}}{\text{Chronological age}} \times 100 = \text{IQ}$$

On average, children score around the 100 mark – sixty per cent of children score between 90 IQ and 110 IQ. A score of 120 IQ or more puts a child into the category of clever; this accounts for about ten per cent of the population. Gifted children in the top two per cent would score between 135 IQ and 170 IQ. An IQ score is always relative, giving the relationship between one child's success at certain tasks and that of others his own age.

But a test can only sample a child's ability at the time he takes it. It measures how well he's taken in what he's learned and how well he can reproduce it for the test there and then. If he's harbouring a cold, for example, then his test result could go down. The benefit of the intelligence test, though, is that it can act as a safety net to help children, particularly clever ones, be recognized for what they are. Otherwise they may be missed and not given a suitable education in which they can work at something like their own level. For example, a child may be mistakenly put in the bottom stream because he's been having trouble at home and begun to do less well at school. There he may lose interest and come up with only average marks. An intelligence test would speedily alert parents and teachers to the fact that he was working well below his capacity and they could then help him to catch up and take his rightful place in the top stream. At the very least, an intelligence test is an objective measure in a sea of opinion, but it must be used with caution.

The very mention of IQ causes many people's hackles to rise; it may seem altogether wrong to measure children's abilities and to make decisions for their future on the basis of that measurement. People question both the standards that are being used and the moral reasons for doing it. The ability to do herself justice in an IQ test depends a great deal on a child's circumstances, such as the use of language in her home and whether she has objects to play with; without the right opportunities, some aspects of intelligence may never develop fully. Is it justifiable, then, to measure intelligence as IQ? The following are some of the questions often asked about IQ:

Is IQ inherited?
It's difficult to say exactly how much of a child's IQ is due to

home background – that is, to environment – and how much is due to heredity. Scientists can't place children in different environments to find out what happens, but nature has provided us with an ideal group for investigation in the form of identical twins. Unlike non-identical twins – who are only as alike as ordinary brothers and sisters, but happen to be born at the same time – identical twins are from exactly the same genetic blueprint. By looking at identical twins who have been brought up in different families, we can see how the different environments have affected two children with the same heredity.

There are problems about this, though, in that the adopting families of both twins may be very similar. Adoption societies usually try to place babies with families as similar to their natural parents as possible. This has the effect of cutting down the environmental differences. But even so, it's clear that there is some genetic inheritance of IQ.

Different statistical methods produce different results. Some say that eighty per cent of intelligence is inherited – which only leaves twenty per cent to be affected by the environment. The most conservative estimates, though, say that inherited intelligence is about thirty per cent of the whole. No doubt the answer lies somewhere between the two extremes, though it is also possible that the amount of inherited IQ varies for different children. Professors Eysenck and Kamin put the opposing points of view on this subject clearly in *The Battle for the Mind*[3].

How does environment affect IQ?
This is a question which this book is aiming to answer. Circumstances (including parents' own efforts) can only affect the latent intelligence available to be developed so it's important to know what makes a difference.

It has been found over and over again that, on average, children from the higher social classes have higher IQs than children from the lower ones. The reason for this is not that richer children are born cleverer, but that they usually enjoy a more educationally positive upbringing. This comes from the attitudes that parents have to their children's intellectual development, and from the standard of provision at home and school. To score a high IQ you need a certain amount of learning, and the children who are in the best position to acquire the right kind will be more likely to fulfil their potentials – which is what the IQ test measures. Evidence from my research (see page 153) on above-average children showed that the two prime aspects of their lives which were most effective in raising the children's IQ scores were their home lifestyles and their educational provision.

The question of race and its relationship to intelligence is probably the most sensitive issue in education today. Some American research, published by Professor Arthur Jensen[4], concluded that black children had lower IQs than white children, while other races scored in between. But this has been severely criticized on both psychological and statistical grounds; the original evidence is now virtually discredited, and even the professor has since changed his mind somewhat. All children are judged individually in this country, regardless of race; each is free to find their own limitations and strengths, through the experience of their own activities.

Can IQ predict success?
Yes, it certainly can predict some kinds of success, like school and university achievement, extremely well – but then so does a child's social background, because these are linked. But the possession of a high IQ alone is not enough to predict success at anything else. The proportion of high-IQ people in the population can easily be calculated, and only some of them could be called successful in worldly terms, while many people with lower IQs are extremely successful.

Personality and outlook are just as important for success as IQ. In fact, if a child is aiming to be a self-made millionaire then a highly developed IQ, which could lead to time spent at a university, can be a positive hindrance. Unless a child will have a busines to go into after university, he could have spent those years building up his own and learning how to cope, instead of practising academic, abstract thinking.

Do boys and girls have different IQs?
It isn't possible to say that one sex is *more* intelligent than the other, but there is evidence for a greater *range* of intelligence among boys. This means that a boy has a greater chance than a girl of being either stupid or gifted. But even after nearly a century of practice, the measurement of intelligence is still so unsure that there may be perfectly good social reasons for these differences, only some of which are known at present. For example, it is known that mentally subnormal boys are far more likely to be institutionalized than girls, possibly because it is more acceptable to have such girls about the house. It may be that just such social reasons are responsible for the relative lack of gifted girls who come to be noticed; their drive to achieve is possibly deflected into other behaviour considered more acceptable for girls.

The main problem with an IQ score is that the figure stands for a whole collection of abilities. It's a bit like saying that your personality is PQ 124 – not really very informative. In fact, the new British Intelligence Scale has given up the idea of a single number IQ, and presents its results as a 'profile' of abilities. Since boys and girls have different rates and types of intellectual development, their results in tests must be seen in relation to the age at which they are measured. The future adult intelligence of girls, for instance, can be predicted when they are between three and six years old, but that of boys has to wait until they are between six and ten. During this later period of development almost twice as many boys as girls show increases in IQ. In addition, girls are generally better with language and boys with numbers, so if a test is made up with a bias towards either of these abilities, then one sex could score more highly. Psychological researchers are still hard at work trying to sort out the influences of heredity and environment in these sex differences, as well as all the other controversies about IQ.

What is the future for intelligence testing?
There are dozens of new ideas coming out of the psychology laboratories about how to measure intelligence. Future test-takers, for example may be:
* listening to clicks in earphones or watching flashing lights while electrodes taped to their temples send brain responses to be analyzed by a computer
* held (as babies) to watch toy cars knocking dolls over while having their heartbeats measured
* tracing a stencil
* describing their daily lives
* organizing dots
* deciding at three years old how they would behave if they were in a game which needed three children and only two wanted to play
* pressing buttons as fast as they can.

Researchers in Russia, where the concept of IQ has never been popular, are aiming to measure 'learning potential'. This approach involves giving children unfamiliar problems and measuring the number of 'prompts' or the amount of coaching they need before they can solve the problems. Here in the West, an attempt is being made to find out the different steps in the reasoning processes, though it sometimes seems as though we know more and more about less and less.

Can parents raise a child's IQ?
With the knowledge we already have it is possible to raise the IQ of an ordinary child by as much as twenty points, and this may increase in the future. But increasing the IQ is not simply a matter of improving a child's environment, by

moving to a clean-air district for example. It comes from the child's own increased attempts to cope with his circumstances – from his experiences in dealing with things and people around him, and seeing what happens. David Lewis describes this process in *You Can Teach Your Child Intelligence*[5] and provides intense training programmes for very keen parents and children to follow.

As an example, non-stop noise – even loud music – played within a baby's earshot can actually be harmful to her IQ development because it interferes with her ability to choose what to listen to. The earliest IQ development occurs in a parent's natural 'conversation' with the baby. The parent often imitates the baby's sounds, then waits for a response from the baby and then imitates that. After a while, the parent may begin to introduce new sounds and words – 'Now I'm going to tickle your *tummy*.' It's the baby's response which is important, and the changes this brings about in her mind. 'Conversation' also helps babies to develop their communication by facial expressions and a sense of trust builds up. As a result of this, they become even more attractive to their parents. To say that children should be seen but not heard would be to limit their intellectual growth; fortunately, it never happens in reality.

The sooner parents begin to foster IQ in a baby's life, the more effective they are likely to be, though development never stops at any age. It's the *rate* of development that changes, and the highest rate is from birth to age two. The longer you wait after that, the harder it is. There are also specially sensitive periods in a child's life when learning takes on a growth spurt. One of these periods appears to end at about age four, and another takes place between the ages of four and eight. The age at which children start school, between four and five, is possibly an age at which there is a low rate of mental growth.

The key problem for parents is in finding circumstances that are sufficiently lively and stimulating for a child, yet not too demanding at his particular point of development. If it's

75

too easy, learning becomes stale; too hard, and it's distressing. But a really good match of ability and challenge brings about such pleasure and increased desire for learning in the child that he will keep going under his own steam, and there's no need to worry about pushing. This is perhaps the art of parenting.

What you can do – IQ

1 Do your best to provide children with toys, drawing paper, musical instruments – anything that they can use to practise their intellectual and artistic skills on – and be as generous as possible. Buy wallpaper lining paper, for example, rather than drawing paper, so that a child can scribble without you feeling that she's just wasting money. Don't stint on giving her things to play and work with. (See opposite for more about toys.)

2 Lead challenging, full lives yourselves. It's important for children to see their parents making use of their own intelligence. Let them join in with your activities – sit down and listen to music sessions together, for example. Any music will do, it's the lively minded listening that's important.

3 Try to be realistic about your child's abilities. Although high expectations can work wonders, if they're too high it can cause damage. When a child can't reach the goal you've set because it's too high, her feelings of self-worth can slump with her failure.

4 Check constantly to see that your child isn't being organized into rigid ways of thinking that are said to be appropriate for her or his sex but which may, in fact, be quite inappropriate for the individual concerned.

5 Think positively and give lots of praise – where it is merited – so that you build up an atmosphere of trust and acceptance in the home. This gives the child the psychological freedom to explore new ideas and know-ledge without the fear of being put-down by sarcasm or sharp correction.

The delight of discovery

Being clever suggests more than an ability to copy, though there's a lot of skill in that too. It's a child's extra urge to find things out and to make things of his own that puts a clever child a cut above the rest. The searching, creative child knows there are many things to be discovered, sorted out and coped with. That's why he works so earnestly at them. First-hand experience is needed to build up impressions and ideas, not just from touching and seeing, but also from rubbing up against another interested mind. The 'silly' ideas and 'stupid' questions of early childhood are a form of exploration and testing which should not just be irritably dismissed – at any rate, not most of them!

The delight of discovery begins at birth – all children know it. But those who are fortunate enough to keep it with them, maybe for life, have the constant yearning to learn, to invent problems and to solve them. Life can be continuously creative and satisfying for children if they get off to the right start. It's no use waiting for school to provide the inspiration for this because it may never happen there. Anyway, it's getting a bit late by then – ways of exploring learning are formed at home.

Toys are important to children, but especially when they can create with them; there is no obligation to follow the makers' instructions, after all. A child may find that building wooden jigsaw pieces into a tower satisfies her more than putting them in the spaces provided. John and Elizabeth Newson describe more toys than you can imagine in their book *Toys and Playthings*[6] and offer lots of ideas for parents.

Of course, children often rate adult activities higher than the toys they're given to play with. Let them become involved with what you are doing about the house, 'working' with you, knocking in nails, cooking or gardening. Try to talk about these things as you do them, connecting up the activities with ideas and then carefully going back over what you've done together. *Supertot* by Jean Marzollo[7] is a little book with lots of suggestions for life with an active toddler, and you'll find quite a few more ideas scattered throughout this book.

Children do not need to be pushed to explore; the average toddler is proof of that. But they do need plenty of experience and the wider the variety of this, the broader the base they will have on which to build their creative awareness. Where variety is difficult to come by naturally, as in a tiny tenth-floor flat, parents have to make an even greater effort to provide it. Television can help. For example, the American television series *Sesame Street* and many British children's programmes are specially designed for this purpose. Then there is the local library service. It is free and particularly useful for toddlers. There are certain to be lots of lovely picture books and you may find pre-school reading sessions are held there. You could take your toddler to art galleries and museums too, but be sure to keep the outings fun and not too long. Trailing wearily round room after room of an exhibition with eager parents is more tiring than inspiring.

It is certainly possible to teach children to use their senses to the full. If they are only aware of part of the world they live in, they will have that much less choice of material to grow with and to create from. Being creative, in however small a way, is demanding and needs time for ideas and products to be developed. Painting on a wet afternoon is fine, but it rather loses its pleasure if a child is constantly being interrupted to do this and that and then finally told to put it all away before he feels it is properly finished. Sometimes, if he is really involved in a piece of work, he may have to go back to it many times over a period of weeks. Also, although there is excitement in discovery, there may also be despair in failure to produce just what he wants, and when parents hear that heartfelt cry: 'I can't do it', they should give their encouragement and interest to see the child through.

In fact, appreciation is a very powerful force on the side of creativity. Treasured works should be displayed where everyone can admire them and not confined to the child's bedroom or put on one side out of the way. Any creative activity is a form of self-expression and what a child makes for herself is more important to her than what an outsider may judge as being her level of achievement. If parents and others are obviously pleased by the result, the child's own satisfaction will be many times greater.

Much of the natural creative spirit that we are born with seems to get squashed out of existence by pressures to conform. For example, a boy may be told that he should not be indoors, working on his cardboard model, but outdoors, playing on his trike with the other children. Why? Because his mother thinks this is the done thing (health doesn't really come into it much). Or a girl may be discouraged from playing with a toy car or engine; her parents feel strongly that this is not suitable for a daughter. Too often, creative activity is thought of only as play, when it is really an important part of learning. In fact, the enjoyment which most children find nowadays in their school work is largely due to its creative aspect. Learning through doing is not only more fun, but more easily remembered and put to use. The child from an open-minded home will probably do better at school than one from a more conventional background.

There are many practical ways of helping a child to express himself creatively, although the most obvious is painting. If a parent makes sure that child, floor and working surfaces are protected from the paint, this will give the psychological go-ahead. Of course, a child must learn to use his tools – too wet a brush or paper that's too thin will impede the creative flow. Water for the paint must be changed often and tissues are a great help for wiping. But remember that your way of seeing is not his – a purple tree is as good as a green one.

Children are sometimes happier making solid things. Masses of cardboard and sticky tape can make complicated dwellings and even towns. Plasticine 'carved' with a blunt knife can produce most impressive results, whilst older primary school children can be taught to use a sharper knife and carve – always away from themselves – in balsa wood or soap. Ready-bought modelling sets are rarely value for money and can take away the thrill of having made something all by themselves. Little children have great fun with glue and round-ended scissors, cutting up bits of cloth and wallpaper which they can stick on cardboard to make a picture. Some like making human figures and some prefer patterns. It can either be drawn out first, or made up as they go along.

Most primary schools now provide creative opportunities, but if you happen to live in the area of one which doesn't you may have to make up for it at home. A school which only dishes up the three R's, with a sprinkling of community singing and crayoning, isn't providing a balanced education. It is also likely to mean that the vital enthusiasm and spirit of which the children are capable either dies away or is kept for out-of-school interests. There are several books which can be useful in this situation. Don't be put off by pictures in them of children's drawings, which always seem outstandingly better than the efforts of your own home; remember that there is something about the printed page that gives glamour to the simplest scribble. See what your local library has, and ask the librarian what else is available.

Exceptionally creative children can be very deprived in an old-fashioned school. As such a child is often the most lively in the class, she may be considered a nuisance by teachers. But this kind of child has something special to offer the world; she is the one who questions what has always been accepted. She is likely to be both sensitive to others and highly critical of herself, as well as having a sense of humour and fun.

If you think you might have such a child in your family, remember that there is a difference between bad behaviour and independence, just as there is between a child who is happier doing things on his own and one who is alone because no-one wants to play with him. A tolerant child is not the same as one who cannot make up his mind about anything. Finally, there is a real difference between the 'product' that is merely cute and one that is truly creative and original. If you're not sure which you're faced with, get whatever expert advice you can. Real creativity shouldn't be missed – for the child's sake and for the benefit of everybody else.

Particularly lively minded children need to have the confidence and the will to take risks, and that is what parents can encourage. The sort of child who will have a go at thinking along different lines from her friends has to have an independent nature and be sure of herself. She's less concerned with what is 'right' or 'wrong' than other children; she goes by her own sense of values, not just by what other people tell her.

Parents direct their children in two ways. The first of these is imperative: 'Be quiet, because I say so.' The second is instructive: 'Be quiet, so you can hear the birds singing.' To help your child towards an adventurous mind, you should rarely use the imperative; it is not often needed, in fact. The instructive approach is far better as it helps the child towards thinking things through for himself which is the very foundation of creative thinking.

There is adequate evidence to show that parents who put strict limits on their children's freedom of action with a constant stream of 'Don'ts', also restrict their curiosity and urge for independent thinking. What may happen as they get older is that instead of being well behaved and obedient, they can become very rebellious, distressed and distressing. 'Don't touch' is probably a parent's most frequently used admonition and its overuse can shut a child's windows on the world, so the best plan is to put the crystal glasses out of a child's reach until she is older. The more creative thinkers come from homes which are less bound by concern for conventional academic success and where the children are given a wide choice of friends and activities.

To be imaginative and creative, a child doesn't have to be

highly intelligent. Great artists, for example, are not specially known for their brilliant intellects. It's only possible to say that whereas a high IQ does not guarantee high creativity, a low IQ certainly works against it.

Discovery on its own isn't very useful; it has to be tied up to what a child knows already and then judged by him for what it's worth. It works like a revolving kaleidoscope – you rummage through what you know and form new patterns, and from those, you can take the creative leap to new ideas. Clever little Henry did just that sort of jump when he was three years old. He couldn't write but he could form numbers, so when he wanted to make a note of his birthday he put 22 on his birthday cards. 'It was *Tues*day,' he explained, so that's why he wrote the pair of 2s.

Parents can teach children to think creatively; the most successful methods use the child's intelligence and feelings together. Mental exercise is the key. When a big business is short of ideas, its chief directors get together for a day or two for a brainstorming session. What they're doing is bombarding their brains with experiences and activities designed to bring out the kaleidoscope effect and judging powers of the brain. It is also a bringing together of everyone's thinking styles, so that right and left brainers, convergent and divergent thinkers can all stimulate each other's thinking.

The first step in teaching a child (or adult) to think creatively is to improve her awareness. You can present a problem to a child which is just within her capacity to have a stab at solving it. Some questions you could put, for example, would be:

For a three-year-old: What can you do with a piece of paper?

For a five-year-old: What would happen if everyone doubled in height?

For a ten-year-old: What do we need to do to feed the world's people?

Here are some real mind-teasers from an American educational system called Syntectics[8]:

* The sky darkening before a storm is like what in the animal world? Why?
* How is a metal base spring like hope?
* An iceberg is like a big idea because . . .?
* If a lake were a table, what would the boats be?

You could try a small-scale creatively brainstorming session, starting with some of these questions or others like them that have no obvious answers. The idea is to stretch the child's imagination as far as possible. You can have a session with one child, but it's more fun with a few. Start by trying to think around possible answers to the questions, making sure that the child feels free to use his imagination. The basic ground rule for this is that no judgement is allowed: there is no right or wrong response. It is a simple rule, but it helps encourage real free choice in a protected atmosphere. Usually, children begin by testing the rule – they can't believe in their good fortune at being free. But if you stick to it, they soon come to recognize and respect their own and others' ideas. Exercising the mind in these conditions enhances the child's feelings of self-worth and personal power. It is in the climate of trust, so essential to creative thought, that he can go ahead with intellectual risk-taking.

Keep up the brainstorming at as swift a pace as the situation will allow, letting imagination strike out more and more widely, questioning and making suggestions again alternately. Children usually love the thrill of the mental chase.

The result of this sort of exercise should be to help children use more and different kinds of ideas in making decisions. But it needs some sensitivity and control by parents. In the same way as you know when children are becoming overtired and in need of sleep, then you will feel when they are getting too excited and you can act to stop the session before they become exhausted and overwhelmed. Sometimes the participants are overcome by giggles, which is OK from time to time, but that needs control too, or the exercise loses its point. If there is the slightest hint of fatigue, then carefully bring the session to a halt using your parental skills. At the end the children should feel on top of the world.

The Bulgarians have a system called Suggestology which works on the principle of pleasure in learning. First of all, the child relaxes her mind, but is ready for action. Then, she and her parents or teacher suggest some understanding of how different ideas and things can be seen together. For example, you could relax with your child and let ideas about wheels, axles, gravity and weight float about in your minds. They may then bump about, setting each other off, and cling together in new ways. It's rather like brainstorming without the tension, and you could end up designing a waggon to the moon.

Away into fantasy

Creative thinking is normally tied up with feelings and needs, desires and fears. Daydreaming is an example of this kind of thought. A little girl playing with her dolls is exploring and sorting out her feelings about family life; the experience is helping her come to terms with her own need for love and care, and she's learning to handle her fantasies at the same time. Great artists, writers and scientists use these child-like mental explorations to help them in their work. Though they can never regain the genuine innocence of childhood, creative people have to be open to fantasy and less hampered by judgements of right and wrong than most of us. This enables them to produce original ideas, which then have to be worked out in detail using adult skills. This is how it seems to work.

1. Preparation

This is the hard work, where the creative person gets to know all he can in his field of endeavour, such as what work has been done previously in it, what techniques are available etc. This is the essential basis for creative thinking.

2. Unconscious thinking

The person now puts all his work aside, shoves everything to the back of his mind and gets on with something else. It's a sort of fermentation process which can go on for minutes or years.

3. Inspiration

An idea can come at any time, but is most likely while drifting off to sleep or waking up. It's very exciting when something is on the way, even if it is only the germ of an idea.

4. Working it out

The process of going back to the drawing board with the new inspiration, logically checking it and following ideas through, is a vital part of making the creative product. This is where real skill and expertise show themselves. Wagner worked on *The Ring* for over twenty-six years. Edison is often quoted as having said that genius is one per cent inspiration and ninety-nine per cent perspiration.

Creative children are particularly independent, and may even prefer not to have a close relationship with their families. They usually come from homes where they are given a lot of encouragement in what they want to do. If a child is truly absorbed in finding out about things, encourage her. There's a noticeable difference between commitment and obstinacy, which parents are usually able to judge. The interests which children have are the best signs of how they're going to grow up. Do they like to make things or to play music, or do they read more than their schoolmates? Even though children's interests change, they usually develop along a recognizable theme. It's worth writing in your diary what interests your child shows and how intense she is about them. If you don't know already, it will give an idea of her real interests and some clues as to how she might make her future.

The future

Clever children are often very concerned for the future of 'spaceship earth'. They are attracted by unknown possibilities and feel challenged to take part in solving problems which have yet to appear. The thought processes needed for sensing and solving future problems are associated with a high level of ability and it is the children who are most concerned about the future in many avenues of life – cultural, scientific, political and educational – who are our most promising natural resource. So it is important to involve clever children in the problems of the world, and not only those of their own community. Unfortunately, much of what is taught in schools is concerned with acquiring and reproducing information and this can blunt a clever child's natural curiosity and desire for change. If a child is limited in his thinking to what's already known, then how is he going to make decisions about what's not known?

The greatest enemy to imaginative thinking and change is conformity. Clever children need exercise for their growing and maturing capacities so that they can have control and confidence in what they can do. It gives them the security to find new knowledge and approach new problems through sharing, rather than hugging facts to themselves in narrow short-sighted competition.

What you can do – for discovery

1   If at all possible, see that the child has enough time and space to be alone with peace of mind, so that she can practise and explore knowledge in a psychologically safe, protected setting.

2   A child has to have the right working materials. For example, Yehudi Menuhin couldn't have been a violinist had his parents not bought him a tiny violin. Make sure there's a generous supply of paper and paints around and egg-boxes and other containers to glue together to make models. Teach children how to work with the minimum of mess, but always give them a place to do it in where mess doesn't matter.

3   Don't interfere all the time, or expect immediate results. A painting a day may not be the best way.

4   Give a lot of support and encouragement. Creativity is anxiety-producing. It has been said that the most creative people are those who can best tolerate anxiety.

5   Be totally accepting of the child's need for privacy and make-believe, and don't let sarcasm creep into your voice.

6   Show by your own lifestyle that discovery is a pleasure. Keep your own interests alive and share them with your child; for instance, you could learn about your district together.

7   Keep your directions positive: 'Do' works better than 'Don't'.

8   Encourage children to use their playthings in new ways. Even babies do it – instead of rattling their rattles, for example, they learn all too quickly to throw them to the ground for the fun of watching you pick them up.

Chapter 4

GROWING UP CLEVER

This chapter is concerned with the kind of family life that is most beneficial to a clever child. The education that babies are given within the family unit is a far greater influence on their intellectual development than they're ever likely to receive again. A baby's first teachers are all the members of her 'family' – not only her parents, but brothers, sisters and other people she sees often. Each family is unique, a small group which acts as a filter for the information that comes to it from the society outside and so provides the child with its own individual culture. Children who are fortunate enough to have a sound home-based educational background are in a much better position to use what their schools have to offer them. But those who are short on home learning are that much more dependent on the educational system.

Take bright little Wendy, for example, who started school without the practice in thinking and questioning that she could have had. Her parents hadn't realized that babies need a rich social life and had kept to a rather strict routine where she was expected to do as she was told. As a result, Wendy hadn't had all the practice she could have had at talking and being listened to, so, though her teacher did try, their earliest conversations went something like this: *Teacher*, looking at Wendy's painting: 'What a lovely picture. Tell me about it.' *Wendy:* 'Cat.' *Teacher:* A nice cat. Is it yours?' *Wendy:* 'Yes.' *Teacher:* 'What sort of a cat is it?' Wendy doesn't answer.

The teacher finds she's not getting very far with Wendy and is concerned about the other twenty-nine children in her class, so she brings her attention for Wendy to a close, and will try again later . . . when she has the time: *Teacher:* 'You've done very well. Would you like to take the picture home?' *Wendy:* 'Yes . . . mmm . . . please.'

By five years old Wendy should have been able and well-practised enough to talk freely about her ideas in choosing the cat for the subject of her painting. She should have been able to bring her past experiences to mind, such as the fact that the cat came to her as a kitten – a birthday present – or the day the cat had kittens. She should also have been able to talk about the future, like when they go to see Grandma at Christmas and they will have to ask a neighbour to feed the cat. The conversation should have gone rather more like this: *Teacher:* 'What a lovely picture. Tell me about it.' *Wendy:* 'This is my cat and her name is Tiddles. Her eyes are yellow and they sort of go up at the corners. But she's not very big.' *Teacher:* 'How old is she?' *Wendy:* 'Well, she's not very old really. We all went to get her from Auntie Mary's when she was a tiny little kitten. She's a lot bigger now, but Mummy says she's not grown-up yet. So, I suppose she'll get bigger.' (and so on . . .)

Another problem of Wendy's was that she didn't quite know how to react when the teacher asked her oblique questions such as 'Would you like to put your painting things away?'. She'd been so used to being told what to do rather than asked to help make her own decisions that in her confusion she didn't always respond to that kind of request. So the teacher had to rephrase it into: 'Put your things away now, Wendy', and then she'd do it. The teacher understood the problem, but she did not have the classroom time to put it right. As a result this clever child did not have a good chance to really enjoy the intellectual life of which she was capable. A child such as this would probably remain unnoticed as an average member of the class. Joan Tough's book *Focus on Meaning*[1] explains these sort of language problems, and how to overcome them, in more detail.

If a newborn baby is to develop into a clever child, he has to have both love and respect from his parents. Love is often taken to be all the emotional support a child needs and respect is sometimes overlooked, but babies are human beings and should be treated as such right from the start. Sometimes, though, so-called respect is misused by parents who attend to the baby's every demand so that their lives revolve around him. For example, when a father said to me: 'I'm often late for work because of Billy', I asked why. 'He talks so much,' said his father, 'that I can't leave till he lets me.' Both parents were happy to explain that it was because Billy was so clever that he had to be listened to; if not, he might get upset. Billy was well accustomed to wielding such power by then – he'd been ruling the family for four years. I couldn't help but feel that Billy would have benefitted from more structure in his life so that he would know, for example, that Daddy set off for work each morning at a certain time, with or without Billy's permission.

Brighter children are more likely to come from homes which are reasonably financially secure. The sense of security and confidence in the parents can be picked up by the child and help her towards gaining the good sense of herself that she needs to become competent. In making the fateful decision to have a child, parents who want the best for her should be clear in their own minds whether they can afford to go ahead. The costs of bringing another individual into the world, especially the first in the family, are very high – many thousands of pounds – even though obviously not all spent at once. The loss of the mother's earnings, even for a while, usually has to be taken into account. The more secure that parents are, both financially and emotionally, the more free they are to concern themselves with the finer points of child care. Parents who are worried or worn out by what they have to do to make ends meet, find it much more difficult to provide the subtle but lasting benefits of easy conversation with their children, the right kinds of learning experiences, enough close contact and a tranquil atmosphere.

One of the most poignant facts to have emerged from many studies of children growing up is that those who start with the same potential are often found to develop and achieve differently. Children from the best homes – educationally – go on steadily to outstrip those from less supportive homes. For example, a major study was conducted across Britain in the 1960s by Dr Douglas[2] to find out how the home lives of 5000 children affected their educational success. The mothers' maternity care was taken into account and their home lifestyle; then the children were tested at eight years old, eleven years old and fifteen years old. Douglas found that the most important influences on the children's school achievement was their parents' interest in them, their hopes for their children and the kind of lives they themselves led. Children who came from homes where parents did not concern themselves greatly with their children's education began to show this lack in their work at primary school. This difference between the educationally supportive and non-supportive homes increased significantly through secondary school. 'This effect,' Douglas wrote, 'extends to pupils of even high ability.' The Plowden Report[3], which surveyed another 3000 families in Britain, found the same effect.

A baby has a better chance to do well when he has both a mother and a father to look after him. Certainly, there are one-parent families where a single adult doing the work of two brings up children beautifully, but unfortunately, that's not always the case. And it's certainly harder work. Even in families where the father's work leaves him little time to see his children, they and their mother can be noticeably supported by the fact that he is at least around. When parents change partners it can have a bad effect on their child's progress, especially during the upheaval of parting; it shows up in school reports with children doing less well than they should. Though no-one can guarantee a perfect marriage, it's definitely unfair to bring children into a shaky one. Having a baby calls for genuine, long-term commitment from both mother and father – it should never be an attempt to put a bad marriage right.

Working mothers

The question of whether mothers of young children should

go out to work seems to result in an extra load of guilt for mothers whatever they do! If they can choose to be full-time home-makers they may feel guilty about not pulling their weight financially, yet if they go out to work, they might be depriving their children of a mother's vital presence at this delicate stage of their lives. Most baby books are written on the assumption that mothers of young children are also housewives and do almost all the child care alone. In fact about forty per cent of mothers of young children now have some work outside the home, and fathers are playing a much more important part in bringing up their children. However, a women's magazine survey (previously mentioned) found, among other things, that only sixty per cent of the fathers had ever put their children to bed, so it looks as if there is still some way to go before parenting is equally shared.

Fortunately, quite a lot of research has now been done to find out the effects of mothers of young children taking jobs or not. Those who stay at home because they want to (and can afford to) bring up normal, happy children. But less keen home-makers can suffer from boredom, especially if they have training which they are no longer using; isolation; fatigue, especially where there are a number of children; and most of all, a need for human contact beyond that of babies. Such conditions can cause young mothers to be unhappy, and *that* is not good for the children. There is some evidence, collected in London by Dr Brown[4], that some employment for mothers outside the home goes a long way towards relieving this distress. But then what will happen to the children?

Considerable evidence collected by the married Doctors Rhona and Robert Rapoport[5] shows that the children of working mothers did not often feel abandoned and unwanted, but were more likely to gain in feelings of independence and respect, with an enriched lifestyle, seeing their mothers as independent rather than dependent women. There does not seem to be evidence of problems for the children caused by their mothers' outside work alone. The real problems in children's lives are more likely to be due to the deprivations of poverty.

A mother's constant presence for the first five years of a child's life is not now seen by psychologists as essential for his well-being and, for the full benefit to the child, fathers should share the work and the pleasure. A baby can be parented at least as well by two people as one, when they have the same style and make sure that he has all he needs in one-to-one contact with either of them. Every couple has to work out their own answer to the question of whether the mother of small children should take work outside the home. Unfortunately, it often seems to be a compromise situation with a 'price' to be paid by the mother, regardless of her choice: mothers in full-time work can get desperately tired, those in part-time work may be passed by for promotion, and those who stay at home unwillingly can suffer from depression and frustration. The question to ask, perhaps, is which 'price' is right for your family.

What you can do – for your family
1 Keep your family to the size and spacing which you can afford, both emotionally and financially.
2 Get close to your baby right from the beginning – at least try. It can sometimes take a while for feelings to develop.
3 Be 'parents' and not only friends to your children. They need some structure in their lives, and to know that they can depend on you within it.
4 Priorities often have to change when you have children. For instance, can you give up some of your house space for the children to use as a playroom? Are you willing to live with the mess they often create?
5 Whether the mother works outside the home or not, the choice must be made by the couple together. Be as open and honest in your discussions as you can, or the underlying resentment in either parent can make family life less than pleasant.

6   Constant absence from children by either parent is not
     good for their healthy, balanced development. If your
     work is all-demanding, you may have to choose between
     cutting it down somewhat or leaving your child in what
     may be in reality a one-parent (or no-parent) family.

First-borns are special

It's still one of the mysteries of psychology why first-born
children in a family are likely to be cleverer and more
successful than the others. The great scientist Francis Galton
stumbled across this interesting fact when he investigated his
fellow members of the Royal Society; a significant majority
of them were first-born children. Since then very many
studies of groups as different as Italian professors, American
astronauts and striptease dancers have shown the presence of
more first-borns in them than could have been expected. Is it
due to their inborn characteristics, or is it the way they're
brought up? If these children who are cleverer than their
brothers and sisters have in fact been treated differently, that
could provide some clues as to how they have been able to get
ahead.

   Being a first-born, or for that matter an only child, has a
big effect on a child's intellectual and personality growth, so
that their intelligence and language ability is often higher
than others. An intriguing study by Eleanor Maccoby and
her colleagues[6] has found that first-borns are born with a
higher level of hormones in their blood than later-born
children, especially if the pregnancies are closely spaced. We
don't yet know, though, what the implications of this finding
are. Most studies of very clever children have found a higher
than chance proportion of first-borns and only children
among them. Sometimes last-borns also do well, but middle-
borns are usually the least successful children.

   Even though these differences in intelligence are real –
when measured across large numbers of people – they cannot
entirely account for the spectacularly high rate of success
among first-borns. A study of school children by Mary

Stewart in 1962[7] looked at the birth order of all the children in secondary schools in a large municipal borough. She found that there was a far higher proportion of first-borns in the grammar schools than in the secondary moderns. This meant that proportionately more of them had passed the entrance exam and would go on to university.

In an important study of 400,000 young men conscripted into the Dutch Army[8], the results showed that the higher a soldier was in his family birth order, the higher his intelligence score was likely to be. It also showed that the larger the family, the lower the intelligence of the younger children was likely to be. Other studies, such as that by Dr Douglas in Britain[2], have also found that children from large families often don't do as well as those from smaller ones. In big, poor families where everyone is crowded into a small home and there isn't enough money for books or leisure activities, there's sometimes too much crowding of all kinds for the children's full mental growth to take place. The greater the strain on a family's resources of attention, care and interest, the less each subsequent child is likely to receive of them; the first-born is always likely to scoop the lion's share.

There's evidence to show that most first-born children do have a different upbringing from the later-born, as described by Sutton-Smith and Rosenberg in a review of all the work in this field[9]. The first-borns are actually only children for a while, which the other children can never be. During this time they can command all their parents' attention, although they must also be guinea pigs for the parents' new child-raising skills. This means that they arrive into a different style of family life from later-born children. New parents – mothers in particular – very often have higher expectations for their first baby than they do for the others. But mothers also give much more help and encouragement to their first child than they do to the later ones, and fathers probably do the same.

The extra attention which the first-born receives – mostly

in his first two years – carries over into his later relationship with his parents, though in different forms. Parents are not quite as easy-going with their first baby as they will be with the rest. Perhaps this is because, as new parents, they are unused to handling babies and so often describe their first-born as less cuddly than the later-borns. Still, in spite of this possible lack of cuddling, first-borns do get more attention than later-borns. They more often model themselves on their parents than later-borns, who are more likely to follow their friends. As first-borns tend to be more considerate too, they can seem to be more 'old-fashioned' and grown-up than other children.

The typical first-born is clever and well behaved. She does her best to please, but may also let you know that she's doing you a favour. She's a bit anxious about life in general and finds it hard to relax, so her leisure time is taken up with fairly 'educational' hobbies such as collecting stamps, from which she can learn a lot. When she's with other children, she usually thinks she knows best, since she sees herself more as a grown-up than a child. Grown-ups are more likely to treat her as one of themselves, so they don't talk down to her, even when she's very tiny. The likelihood is that she takes more responsibility than the other children of the family. This seems to work out, since she's usually a more 'responsible' child. The best card she has to play is her own success; the first astronauts to set foot on the moon were all first-borns, and it's very likely that the top of the class will be one too.

Only children may do even better at school and in intelligence tests than first-borns as they often aim higher and are more ambitious. But they are more dependent on being told what to do and on parents' and teachers' opinions. Although it seems at odds with this dependence, they have a higher level of self-confidence.

It's often said that middle children have to struggle to keep their end up in a family, and this is true. They do receive less attention than any others in the family, and seem to feel this lack for much of their lives. When they're little, they'll often go to great lengths to make their presence felt, even if it results in punishment. They can be particularly quarrelsome and obstinate, and are often the least popular members of the family. It's unlikely that they will ever do as well as the first-born, since their drive to succeed is usually much lower.

Children's popularity with their friends is also affected by their position in the family. First children, so grown-up and sometimes 'know-all', are the least popular. Middle children usually have as many friends as they want, but last-born children hit the top of the popularity ratings – their teachers show them the same warmth as friends of their own age do. Right through from kindergarden, last-borns are always the most attractive to teachers, and first-borns the least attractive.

What you can do – position in the family
1   Space your family so that each child can get plenty of attention when they are very tiny. With generous spacing between each birth, say three or four years, each baby can almost be a first-born for a while, though children born closer together do benefit more later on from each other's companionship.
2   Try especially hard to give the later-born children what you gave the first. Obviously this is not entirely possible, but you can try to avoid the snare of giving relatively less and less attention to each child that comes. To make sure, you could keep a rough written checklist on what you do for each one.

Clever children's friends
Some people say that clever children don't make friends of their own age easily because they get bored and frustrated with children who have a lower lever of understanding. Although there may be a problem when a clever child is very much in advance of his age group, this isn't usual, nor is it unsolvable if it arises. If clever children don't seem to want

to make friends with others of their own age, it can be for two reasons. The first is their high level of self-sufficiency, which means that they're happier on their own for longer than other children, but the other reason is that they may have been 'put off' playing with other children by their parents' disapproval.

Whether they're clever or not, children in mixed ability classes at school pick friends across a wide mental range. And it's the same at home – clever children will normally play happily with less clever children. But sometimes parents give their children the idea that they're quite different (if not superior) and expect them to spend their time more purpose-fully than in ordinary play. These messages are sent in very subtle ways. For example, a mother might say: 'Oh, you want to play with Johnny . . . he's a bit quiet for you, isn't he?', or she may just pull a disapproving face at the mention of children who don't meet with her approval.

Clever children usually have sympathy, adaptability and compassion in abundance, and don't usually choose to be without friends. Left to themselves, they will have the same number and depths of friendships as other children at school, but they're sometimes less eager to spend time playing at home. The reason is often that there's so much they want to do after school. Many clever children use that time to enjoy their hobbies, or they may practise a musical instrument. After that, there's tea, maybe a little television, and then bed: another day gone.

It's important for all children's emotional development, and therefore their intellectual development too, to have friends. Children who haven't got many friends find it much harder to grow up as well-balanced adults. Many psychologists have found that children learn a lot about how to behave and cope with life through their friends.

Friends help children to see life from another's point of view, so that they can learn more about concern for others, and friends do have similar problems with grown-ups. Criticism and support are often more acceptable to a child when they come from friends; parents' fears of the bad influence of friends aren't usually justified. The rough and tumble of learning to make and break their own relationships helps children find out about themselves. It also teaches the skills they need for working and living with other people. And that's something which is as important for clever children as any others.

Younger children enjoy playing with older children and usually imitate them, so older children can often be very good teachers for younger ones. Some schools take advantage of this, especially when children first start school, by putting older ones in charge. The old-timers can then teach the newcomers about how to behave in school, not to mention helping them tie their shoelaces.

There are children who can be described as 'socially gifted'. They have lots of friends and seem to be unusually sensitive in understanding other children's feelings. Such children very often turn out to be leaders, though they aren't necessarily more intelligent than their followers.

What you can do – friends

1   From about a year old, make sure your child mixes with other babies. They won't play together yet, but they'll get used to having each other around.

2   Help your toddler learn to share toys and adult attention by explaining this patiently and gently, as necessary. The message will come through in time.

3   Respect your child's choice of friends, though it may be surprising, or even hard at times. It's part of your respect for your child as a person.

4   Try not to be too protective; children learn about other children from their own mistakes, and don't usually appreciate an adult's point of view as to who's worth being friends with.

5   Clever children do take special pleasure in a meeting of minds. If your child is really without equally able children to play with in her local group, try to see that she gets to know one or two even if they live further away.

About sleep

Clever children are sometimes said to need less sleep than other children. If this were true, then parents of clever children could anticipate it and learn how to deal with it, but as yet there isn't any evidence to support the idea. However, there is plenty of evidence to show that children's sleeping habits are very much influenced by their parents' approach to bringing them up.

As they grow older, both the length of time children sleep and their wakefulness during the night become less. In this respect children do vary, though, not only as individuals but in terms of their families. When they were studying the daily routines of babies in England, Lawson and Ingleby[10] found that what was considered to be 'normal' sleeping time varied by a difference of hours between families. 'Normal' waking-up time for toddlers was seen as any time between 6 and 10.30 am, and the time for going to sleep varied from 5.30 to 11 pm. They noticed that first-born babies were put to bed less often than later-born babies, and they slept less too. There were also social class differences; the higher the social class, the longer the baby was expected to sleep, and both going to sleep and waking were earlier in the day. Other researchers, such as Richards in Cambridge[11], found that parents were not able to alter children's sleep patterns no matter what they did – the children just seemed to be born with a particular sleep pattern.

Parents' feelings about what constitutes a sleep problem depend very much on their attitudes. If they are relatively easy-going in their approach, the child may be given toys and books to play with and allowed late bedtimes, and it is less likely that a problem will develop. But if they feel strongly about their responsibility to instil good habits, then the child may be required to lie still, stop reading, be quiet etc. by six o'clock. Lawson and Ingleby found a significant proportion of parents in Britain who did just that every night. If the child wasn't ready for sleep by then, they were likely to treat this as a problem.

In fact, most children have sleep problems at some time, and about half of all parents worry about whether their children are getting enough sleep. Children tend to have problems with sleep at particularly anxious periods in their lives, such as the birth of another baby in the house, starting school, separation from mother or strained relations between parents. Babies' sleep patterns affect their growing relationship with their parents. For example, if a baby doesn't sleep as expected, parents may become frustrated and pass angry feelings back to the infant.

Unfortunately, some children are just poor sleepers from the time they are born. These children, perfectly normal in all other respects, may have some history in common. They're often born after long labours, and have been rather fussy and wakeful from birth. On average, they spend less time in bed than other children, but it doesn't seem to do them any harm. Parents of poor sleepers may try many things, such as changing feeding times or giving more cuddling and attention, but it usually doesn't influence the sleeplessness. Not even the parents' attitudes towards the child seem to make any difference. What can happen is that a constant battle ensues, in which everyone, apart from the baby, suffers from lack of sleep. Some parents alter their lives to fit in with a baby's choice of sleep times – for example, getting up at 3 am for playtime. That's dedication – or madness, depending on your point of view!

What you can do – sleep
1   Keep bedtime as calm and regular as possible. About half of all children between the ages of one and two make a great fuss at bedtime; try to ride the storm calmly, being both reassuring and firm.
2   All children wake several times during the night and fall asleep again. Don't go into your child's room constantly to see if he's alright, or you may disturb his natural rhythm and set up expectations and demands. For instance, each time you go in, he may wake and want to

be taken into your bed. Don't start this, or you'll regret it.

3 Try to judge how much sleep a child really needs, rather than going by a book that says how much time he 'should' sleep.

4 Put just enough (but not too many) interesting toys in the cot for a child to play with when he's wakeful; you can tie them on to the side when he's little. Provide more involving things, like cloth books, when he gets older. (See pages 41 and 53-4 for cot toys.)

5 Try not to make an issue of sleep; it will only make matters worse.

6 Parents need time to themselves too. Children can understand from an early age that once they are comfortable and have something to do in bed, then you have a right to a breather.

Parents with problems

Clever children are particularly sensitive to other people's feelings, especially those of their mothers and fathers. So, when there's some tension brewing at home, they may be the first to know about it. But children are affected differently by what they feel, and they have their ups and downs, too, which can make it difficult to tell how they're being affected. Just like adults, a child may find his problems weighing heavy one day but perk up the next.

Although there are children who seem to be able to cope when their parents aren't getting on well together, for many it can disrupt their lives so that they become unhappy and are then called 'problems'. Boys seem to be particularly sensitive to parental problems, or at least they react to them more than girls, as an in-depth study on the Isle of Wight directed by Professor Rutter[12] discovered. It's the constant pull of strained relationships that does most of the damage, but sometimes parents can also blame their troubles on the child, who is merely reacting to their personal problems, and so the situation goes from bad to worse. 'If it wasn't for

Janice,' they might say, 'we'd be happy.' But it's more likely to be the parents' behaviour that affects the children rather than the other way round, so that when the parents' lives become more harmonious, then their children's behaviour, and their performance at school, very often improves.

The way parents feel about each other affects the way they bring up their children. For example, when a child is punished in a loving, accepting home, then the child understands what it's for, without heavy emotional overtones. But when parents are under strain, the quality of their general care may suffer, so that punishment is given out arbitrarily, confusing the child, who can't always see what he's done to deserve it. Sometimes it swings the other way, though, and parents under strain can become over-protective.

Children most often react to strained relationships at home in one of two ways:

By becoming over-anxious

This anxiety often comes out as aggression, in the form of bad behaviour. Demonstrations of anger can be learned by even the tiniest baby, who may discover that it's only when she gets really worked up to screaming point that she gets the attention she wants, while silence or whimpering get her nowhere.

By becoming safety valves

Children can draw attention away from the real problem of family stress and on to themselves. They can, for example, seem to be unwell. Most parents recognize the tummy-ache before school as a sign of tension, but other more serious problems such as asthma or diabetes can also be signs of stress, and often vanish when the stress goes.

Unfortunately, parents have been known to justify their child's bad behaviour by claiming it's because he's clever, saying that it's only natural for him to be disturbed in this 'mediocre' world. So when a clever child has a temper tantrum, or disturbs the other children in class, it's said to be excusable because he's bored. Frustration and boredom – which are common to most children at times – should never be used as a licence for bad behaviour. When clever children have behaviour problems, the likelihood is that there are reasons behind it, and these need attention, not excuses.

A warning for parents

As Charlie Brown, one of the most prominent philosophers of this century, put it: 'There's no heavier burden than a great potential.' Sometimes you can try too hard to produce a child whose excellence brings credit to you. Pride in one's children's achievements is only right and good, but should you find yourselves thinking and talking of little else, then it's time to sit back and consider why. Parents can live 'through' their children by pushing them to reach standards they never achieved themselves, either because they weren't capable of it or because they didn't have the opportunity.

It's impossible for a child to live up to his parents' expectations all the time, and sometimes he will let them down. These little failures can give his confidence a knock, which won't matter too much in the ordinary way of things. But when the child is under too much pressure to succeed, his lack of confidence can either make him try exceptionally hard to please or perhaps just make him give up. A child can be too 'good', which may cause him to harbour feelings of resentment, maybe for the rest of his life.

It's important for a child to have the freedom and self-esteem to fail, yet know that he's still OK in his parents' eyes; it's all part of learning. Try to bring about an atmosphere at home in which the child feels secure and accepted for himself, whatever he might do. This doesn't mean removing all discipline – parents have a right to live too – but being aware of what your child is able to cope with. Expectations should not be too high or too low, but just right.

What you can do – family problems

1   Be clear in what you are directing the child to do and how you feel about it. Does 'Behave yourself' really

mean 'Be quiet'? If it's quiet you're after, then say so and say why.

2 Each parent should avoid giving instructions that contra-dict the other's; it confuses a child and makes him anxious, so try to be consistent.

3 Respect your child's integrity; trust him to mean well.

4 Keep the atmosphere of the home as tension-free as you can, for example, by keeping parental arguments out of children's hearing.

5 Reassure the child of his rightful place in the family, and tell him this in words of one syllable.

6 When you're wrong, admit it. Your saving face is always less important than the child's feelings and what he's learning from you about life.

How competence develops

Competence is an essential part of a clever child's learning. Though it's difficult of describe, we all know it when we see it! Being able to cope means taking the right action at the right time; it means making things happen, as well as seeing them through in the right way. Children learn how to be competent, and learn the self-esteem that goes with it, in their families.

Babies soon learn the effects they can have on their world, and at the same time begin to learn how to value themselves. During his first year, a baby comes to realise that he exists independently of other people and that he's different from them; it's then he begins to get a glimmer of under-standing of the word 'me'. That's why parents should answer the baby's crying and calls as much as they can, because his growing sense of self-worth comes from his communication with others. Though a child only really sees himself as an individual member of the family from about three years old, he's been striving to get there for a long time. When you're two years old, you're small and unable to think very far ahead so the best stab you can make at independence is just to say 'no' to everything.

It's when the baby begins to recognize familiar people from strangers, at about six months, that you can see his first stirrings of independence. Soon he begins to crawl off and explore around when he's confident that Mummy and Daddy will be there all the time. Babies start exploring when they're ready; parents can't push them into it, but they can pave the way. Play with your baby and make encouraging noises when he reaches out for something; tell him how well he's doing all the time – it gives him confidence to try a bit more. Wherever he is, the room has to be reasonably baby-proof, or parents spend their time saying 'No, don't touch', which isn't good for anyone. Sometimes, parents' own feelings of insecurity won't allow them to help their baby find his way around. How often over-anxious mothers say: 'Don't do that; you'll hurt yourself'. Whether that's really a likelihood or not, it certainly puts a brake on the baby's exploring for a while. Adults who let the baby know that he's helpless and useless can undermine both his confidence and his ability to use his inner resources when he needs them; in effect, they can slow up his thinking this way. Every step forward a baby takes, every new friendship, every meeting with a new idea can add to his feelings about himself and his growing competence. Children's intellectual development is very closely tied to their emotional state; parents who help them to cope are also helping them to do better in life. This isn't only a matter of giving them confidence in themselves, but means showing them ways of doing things and involving them in the process.

Here are two examples of the way competence-building works. While waiting for a prescription to be made up by the chemist recently I was able to watch a complete interaction of a mother and her little boy of about four years old showing how to cut down a child's communication skills. They came to my notice when the child demanded sweets very persistently. At last his mother gave in, then ignored him while he tore off the wrappings and dropped them on the proud shop-keeper's clean floor. Then the little boy tried to talk to her, but at first she wouldn't listen. 'Speak up,' she said eventually, 'I can't hear you when you mumble.' So the child spoke up . . . 'Don't shout,' she said, 'I'm not deaf.'

Four-year-old Mary's problem had a happier ending. She'd been given a simple train set for her birthday, but it took up all the floor space in her room. Mary and her parents put their heads together; father, who'd twisted his ankle on it, wanted it put away at night, mother, who had a feeling for tidiness, tended to agree with him, though she understood Mary's feelings too. It was Mary who, at the last minute, saw that moving the bed along the wall would solve the problem. Her initiative was rewarded by her parents' sincere expressions of delight at her competence, and she then had the train set out all the time. She'll use her head again when she needs to – clever girl.

What you can do – competence

1   Give your baby lots of opportunities to try out his new coping skills. 'Educational' toys like putting rings on a peg are useful for babies; later on, friendships become more important, so see that he has companions and meets people. John and Elizabeth Newson's book *Toys and Playthings* (see Reading list) is very helpful on choosing educational toys.

2   Encourage a child to understand what he's doing and why; it develops his self-understanding. You can do this from a very early age by talking about what you and he are doing, and trying different approaches such as 'Let's see what happens if you shake it'.

3   Reward good behaviour when it happens, rather than simply giving in to constant demands to gain a moment's peace. For example, when your child's been noticeably good by 'helping' with the washing-up, reward him with a kiss or something nice and say thank you. But if he screams for sweets at the supermarket checkout, where they are usually temptingly on display, don't give in; it only encourages him to scream again next time.

4   Keep the idea of learning as a pleasure, so that you don't use the word 'no' more than you can help. Encourage the baby's natural feeling for exploring, and take part in his explorations yourself.

5   Little children can be given simple tools so that they can learn how to use them under supervision. Competence in common, potentially dangerous activities, like handling hammers and nails and knowing how to swim, is far better than trying to put the damage to rights afterwards.

6   Babies need balance in their interests. Mothers should try to get a free and easy relationship going between themselves and their babies by the time they are a year old. The baby will then have the confidence to let his mother out of his sight and take more interest in other things – otherwise, you could end up with a two-year-old nagger.

Chapter 5

THE THREE Rs

Reading

Only a small part of the information necessary for learning to read comes from the printed page; most of it comes from listening and talking. Parents can help to bridge the gap between spoken and written language since the closer the child's spoken language is to what she sees on the printed page, the easier it will be for her to read. Bombarding a child with speech can be too much – it's quality and her participation that counts.

You can encourage your child to be clear in what she says for example, by trying to get her to put her message in a different way. The mental exercise will help her to extend her thinking. This talk between three-year-old Barbara and her mother may not seem much, but it shows that her ideas are getting a little clearer: *Barbara:* 'The milkman's come with the milk.' *Mother:* 'Ah, but where did he get it from, I wonder.' *Barbara:* 'Well, you know, cows. Well, they do it.' *Mother:* 'What do cows do?' *Barbara:* 'Well, you get milk from them.' *Mother:* 'And then?' *Barbara:* 'Well, it goes into bottles and we get it.' *Mother:* 'Tell me about how it gets into the bottles.' *Barbara* (thinking quickly): 'The milkman squeezes it in.'

The two most important aspects of talking with a child are the topic of the conversation and who's participating – the topic must be interesting to the child and the adult should be someone who is important to him. Parents must really listen and respond carefully. For example, John, who was nearly three, was playing with his toy cars on the floor while his father watched from his armchair. After a while John said: 'That car's broken.' *Father* (coming over): 'Let's have a look. Oh! it's not broken, it's a lorry and the platform tips up. See how it goes.' *John:* 'Let me, let me.' *Father* (handing it back): 'Find something for the lorry to carry, so you can see how it works.' *John* (showing his new learning): 'This lorry's mine and I'm not going to.' *Father:* 'What will you do then?' *John* (keeping his end up): 'I'm putting this lorry on top of another lorry.'

John had got the idea of using the lorry for carrying things; he'd shown his growing independence by refusing his father's advice, then gone one better by having the lorry itself carried. His father couldn't help laughing with him at John's delight in his cleverness. Printed words aren't quite the same, psychologically speaking, as spoken ones. They are much more complicated to interpret. When you read, the translation from print to meaning happens in two ways. The letters on the page have first to be understood as sounds and then as words. Your eyes dart about seeing how the letters lie on the page and sneaking a look at what is coming next, while your mind is working out what those collections of marks mean. The first thing a child has to learn in reading is what to 'sound' and what to ignore. Reading isn't only a matter of decoding marks into spoken language, though; it's a skill for communication. Each person has his own way of using and controlling this skill.

When a beginning reader reads aloud to you, don't just listen to see whether she's doing it correctly or not, so that you can put her right. Listen to what she says; then, when she's wrong, let her join in so that she learns self-correction; don't say 'No, you don't say the "d" properly in Wednesday', instead say something like 'Try the word again, as you say it usually.'

Sometimes children make a stab at a word they don't know, using the rules from the other words they do know, such as when a toddler says 'I didded it.' Though this approach may produce the wrong results in our illogical English language, it shows the beginnings of an awareness that print carries a message. It also shows that the child is using her intelligence to learn to read and such an effort should be warmly encouraged. Parents have to reassure beginners that reading is for pleasure, and have to help them to want to learn to read for themselves. Reading aloud to little ones helps them to get that feeling, from the very earliest weeks – even if they don't understand a word. A small child gets to know the rhythm and structure of written language from this, so that when she gets to read for herself, she'll be better at the anticipation part of the reading job. Book language is really something special.

A recent study in Scotland by Dr Margaret Clark[1] on children who could read fluently before they started school, brought out some features of early reading which parents should know. These children, who had learned at home, were better at reading silently than children who had learned to read in front of the class at school. They took more pleasure in it and were also better at spelling, since all the time they were learning to read, their parents had helped them to write too. They had been given blackboards and chalk to work with, and lots of paper and pencils. As a result, they had become sensitive to the way words are made up of letters, and to how they should sound, and so they made a great effort to get it right.

When children are learning to read, and as they move on to tackle harder books, they will progress better if they have instant assistance from an interested adult to help them when they get stuck. This is where parents have the edge over teachers; while a teacher simply can't provide that kind of service to every one of her class when they need it, parents – or any other adult who's minding the child – can do it.

Children who learn to read early and with pleasure usually have parents who feel the same way about the joy of reading. It's not a matter of money or social class – with our free library service – it's a matter of what parents do together with their children. Where written and spoken language are experienced by a child as everyday happenings, in a warm and accepting family, her education will have been given a great start.

111

Should parents teach reading?

Many parents are anxious that if they teach their children to read before starting school it will cause problems later on. Some feel it will interfere with the child's normal development, and others that the school will look less favourably on their child. In fact, parents often don't tell the school that the child can read as they feel embarrassed about it. Agatha Christie's parents refused to let her read before the age of seven as they thought it wasn't good for young children. But she, being a clever child, wrote in her autobiography that she taught herself before the age of five.

The idea of 'Reading readiness' – that if you teach a child to read before she's 'ready' she will suffer from emotional problems – has been around for some time. This idea took hold in America for many years, so that some school areas still try to prevent children from learning to read until they are seven years old. At the opposite extreme, Doman's *Teach Your Baby to Read*[2] had some babies recognizing words on cards before a year old – though there seems to be little value in this exercise. From a common sense point of view, it seems ludicrous to say that children aren't ready to read when they can already read fluently.

Teachers vary in their reaction to the news that a five-year-old can read. Some are excited, and see it as giving the child great scope, but others are either indifferent or else feel it will leave the child bored. Some primary teachers unfortunately aren't very interested in a child's learning experiences outside school, feeling that their education begins when they enter the school's portals.

Parents usually know which school their child will go to when she's five, and can sound out the school's attitude. Not that they should prevent a child from reading, even if the school disapproves, but they can help to smooth over her entry to school. Parents who don't give the teacher the information she should have, for whatever reason, are not helping her to do her job properly. It also means that the teacher learns not to trust parents. Obviously the changeover has to be handled with tact, but if your child can read, then say so.

If a child isn't interested in reading, then there's no point in forcing her to try before she starts school. It's important that the child's early experiences of reading be successful; a child learns to read by reading and wanting to read more. Parents' anxieties about reading can cause children to feel failures, which may prove to be an emotional drag on further learning. It's extremely unlikely that a sighted child will have physical problems in learning to decode printing, but there may be other reasons for difficulty with reading.

Dyslexia

Clever children can have difficulty in learning to read and write. The word which is often used to cover the whole range of such problems is dyslexia or word blindness. Interpretations of this condition range from the mildest difficulty with reading to very specific problems such as the child's inability to translate the visual symbols on the paper – the letters of the alphabet – into words. But of all children with reading problems, those with dyslexia are only a small minority. To be dyslexic a child must not only have difficulty in reading, but must also have an average or superior intelligence and normal functioning senses. Other members of a dyslexic child's family are often found to have the same problem and the disorder is most frequently found in boys. The actress Susan Hampshire, who is dyslexic herself, has suggested in her book *Susan's Story*[3] that 12.5 per cent of all children are dyslexic to some extent.

There are some fairly clear signs of dyslexia which parents can look for if they are worried about their child's reading level, and the earlier they are spotted the better are his chances of improvement. Though children who learn to read normally can also come up with similar problems, they will get over them and make good progress, but the dyslexic seems to get stuck and can't get on without help.

Many sufferers seem to have difficulty in interpreting the letters of a word in the right order. The word 'saw', for example, may be read as 'was', and the word 'no' as 'on' or 'dog' as 'god'. You may find that your child is writing as though looking in a mirror, so that 'dog' then becomes 'gob'. Such children need a lot of patient teaching. By sheer hard work a dyslexic child may learn that p-i-g spells pig, only to forget it all the next (if not the same) day. Sometimes a dyslexic child's spelling can be so bizarre that even the most empathetic reader can't make it out. These spelling mistakes often carry on into adult life, even when the person has learned to read with useful skill. Dyslexic children usually have difficulty in working out laterality – left/right and up/down – and they can't refind their place on the page if their attention is lost for a moment. They may have very poor short-term memories, forgetting what you've just told them, often can't seem to be able to keep still and tire very easily. As toddlers they may have been late in learning to fasten buttons and put their clothes on properly.

Reading difficulties in clever children are not always due to dyslexia though. They may have problems with reading for any of the following reasons:
* Problems with speaking, hearing or seeing
* Emotional disturbance, such as insecurity
* Prolonged illness
* Discouragement
* Poor teaching

Unfortunately, whatever the reason, poor reading skills can spill over to affect a child's learning in other areas, such as arithmetic, or all round so that she feels low about her general ability to learn. She may also take to misbehaving, possibly opting out of classroom projects, which isolates her even further. Clever children are particularly good at hiding the basic reading problem. They can find a thousand excuses such as going to the loo just when you want them to read, finishing their maths, losing their glasses and so on. This can work well in a busy classroom, but of course it makes the child's situation worse by delaying the help they so badly need.

It is often impossible to find the root cause of dyslexia. There is a theory that certain parts of the brain which deal with symbols and laterality simply fail to mature normally. In any case, the best anyone can do is to try to relieve the immediate problems. It is also important to help a dyslexic child realise that his difficulty is not a stigma. There are no easy cures available and though educational gadgets may offer variety there is no substitute for a specially trained teacher – with infinite patience. But, because of the shortage of teachers, parents may find that they have to shoulder most, if not all, of the burden themselves. Here are some ideas about what to do if you think your child may be dyslexic:

* Consult the school, who may be sympathetic and offer help.
* If the school indicates that in their eyes your child is simply 'thick' or 'spoilt', ask for him to be tested by an educational psychologist. Your city or county hall should be able to help you. If there is difficulty, you could have your child assessed privately.
* Contact either or both of these dyslexia organisations:

The Dyslexia Institute
133 Gresham Road
Staines, Middlesex
(Tel: 59498)

The British Dyslexia Association
4 Hobard Place
London SW1
(Tel: 01-235 8111).

They can provide assessment, advice, teaching help and an understanding ear. They will tell you the truth too.

Even when a child who has difficulty with reading is referred to as dyslexic by a psychologist or teacher, it does not mean that he can't improve over time. Any child with normal hearing and seeing facilities can learn to read reasonably well, even though his development may be slow or uneven, and dyslexic children usually have good compre-hension to help them. W.B. Yeats, the poet, and Hans Christian Anderson were both dyslexic. Some children, with great grit and determination, go on to extensive study for professions such as medicine and dentistry. But others will always have difficulty in writing a note for the milkman or reading a timetable.

There are some home exercises you can try, but if in doubt do seek the help of an expert; not all parents have the patience of saints. Though learning to read is best encouraged by the pleasure it brings, it is likely to be hard work for the dyslexic. The adult in charge has to provide lots of breaks, a variety of approaches and lavish encouragement. Try reading one page of a book (of a suitable level) together, then talk about what you have read. Ask the child to imagine what comes next before he goes on, so that he has to think forwards. Other points to remember are to listen to the child reading without correcting him for as long as you can and do not offer false praise. Make spellings so easy that he's bound to succeed. Finally, though, work along with trained help rather than trying to do your own thing with the child as an extra. Concerted effort is important.

The methods schools use

There have been no less than thirteen innovations in teaching children to read in Britain within the last quarter century. The most noticeable was the Initial Teaching Alphabet (ita). In this a new alphabet was devised so that children could spell the words the way they sounded, like 'tuf' instead of tough. This was found to be a help to slow learners, but did not benefit clever children. Most schools have now dropped it. There have also been a variety of colour-coded teaching designs and even programmed learning using machines, but these proved too expensive for most schools. These are the three basic teaching methods:

Look and say (whole word or sentence)
The idea behind this method is to establish a relationship between what the child sees (and remembers) and what he

hears so that he forms a chain of mental connections the way adults do when they read. The child is presented with a word or phrase by the teacher and repeats it aloud; the words the teacher chooses are those she thinks will interest the child. Teachers usually ask children to write the words at the same time to build up a feeling for them by the movements made in writing. A child can get on very quickly and get more pleasure from reading this way, but the method often produces poor spellers and even good silent readers may later be seen making movements with their mouths and throats.

Phonic method

Here the child is taught to recognize sounds from letters and to make them up into words like c-a-t spells cat. It begins by emphasizing words which follow well defined rules, then goes on to introduce less regular words like 'would'. The material to be learned has to be carefully organized, for example into what teacher's call 'magic e' or same-sound letter patterns such as meat and peep; soft or hard letter sounds such as sage and gate; and what happens when you add an 'e' to words such as care and fire.

The problem with this method is that it is less immediately rewarding to children, so they are less keen to learn than with the Look and Say method. But it does make good spellers and possibly produces a better understanding of English language.

Eclectic methods

Many schools take what they want from the above two methods and mix them as they see fit. In fact most parents and teachers do this to some extent. It is important to realise that no one method of reading can suit all children. Reading is entirely a matter for the individual as it isn't just a matter of decoding marks on the page, but a constructive thinking process. Reading 'between the lines' is part of normal, meaningful reading.

The fluent reader has abandoned the word by word or

117

symbol by symbol approach. She skims the lines reading for meaning and looking for familiar sentence structures. Gradually her response to what she sees becomes automatic and she only hesitates to decipher slowly when she comes to an unfamiliar word or sentence structure.

Try and stop them!

Clever children who learn to read when they are still toddlers often seem to do so by dragging their unwilling parents in as teachers. Very few parents actually set out to teach reading to uninterested infants. Certain children want to learn and parents are simply going along with it as well as they can.

Right from the beginning these early readers use their new skill to extend their knowledge – sometimes by means of newspapers and sometimes by books. If you read a 'quality' paper at home, it's a good idea to buy a simpler one for a while, for your early reader to practise on. Make sure you take your child to the local library and show her how to choose books. Most libraries have a special advice librarian for children, who can be very helpful.

Our Victorian grandparents knew the pleasure of reading aloud to each other. There is every reason to go on doing this with children even when they can read for themselves. The extra benefit is that now the child can read to you – then talk about what either of you have read. But by five years old a clever child is beginning to get pleasure from reading alone. Give him time and peace to get to know books by himself as well as enjoying them together.

Clever children catch on to the idea of reading from many places. They see words on television, for instance – advertisements often show a word, then say it for the viewer. Later on, a child may see the advertised product on the supermarket shelves or in the kitchen, and can again practise looking at the name and saying it. Some children learn from the titles of gramophone records, by memorizing the whole title and reading the simpler words. Words and sounds are everywhere; clever children very soon begin to put them together.

118

What should they read?

Local libraries and schools very often group children's books in a way that adults think are suitable for children of certain ages. Some schools and libraries will only allow children to pick books out of the age-group that has been earmarked for them. It may be difficult to persuade a school to allow an infant access to the junior bookshelves, but with a parent's membership card, there's no problem at the local library. Clever children who can read fluently are often interested in much more than children's books can offer them.

Let children choose to read what they want. If they don't understand the book they've taken out, they'll either skip the hard parts or take it back. If a five-year-old picks up Tolstoy, does it really matter if he has to take it back the next day as a mistake? After all, we learn from our mistakes. But such clever children may merely be irritated by the simplified vocabulary of children's books for their own age group.

What you can do – reading

1   Talk and listen to your baby from the time of birth.
2   Tell him stories.
3   Show him pictures and talk about them together.
4   Encourage him to talk about what he's been doing.
5   Point out words wherever you are – on television and in the street.
6   Try to use proper sentences when talking to him.
7   Teach him nursery rhymes; stress the rhythm, sing and do the actions.
8   Teach colour names.
9   Encourage him to speak clearly.
10 Board games like 'Snakes and Ladders' help coordinate eye and hand movements.
11 Tap out simple rhythms together.
12 Put up the names of things, printed in large letters on cards, over everyday objects – like SINK on the sink or BED over his bed.
13 Above all, listen to your child's attempts at reading.

The more he reads the better. Once he's finished a book give him another, especially one with pictures which are big, clear, up-to-date and relevant to him.

14 Take it easy. Over-anxious parents can put a child off reading. If you are in any doubt as to a child's readiness to read, wait till you can discuss it with his teacher. Sing and tell him stories instead.

15 Although written for teachers, *Framework for Reading* by Joan Dean and Ruth Nichols[4] has many ideas in it which can help parents, especially in the second half of the book.

Writing

Reading and writing skills don't develop together, they have different psychological beginnings. Being able to read means to sort out letters and their meanings and to remember them; being able to write means fine control of finger and arm movements, and the skill to reproduce letters. Some very young clever children may even be able to read by three years old, but they won't be able to write then. A five-year-old may read fluently, but still find difficulty in tying his own shoelaces.

The beginnings of writing come from painting and drawing. Sit down with your child and show her how pleasant it is to draw as soon as she can barely grasp a crayon. Then you can print in big letters underneath her drawing what she says it is. In time she'll start to go over your printing with her crayon.

When a child has a vocabulary of about a hundred words she should be given a special notebook with a letter written on each page in alphabetical order. Then when she's stuck on how to write a word she can usually show you the first letter and you can help her with the rest.

Some schools try to coordinate the learning of reading and writing; this can make life difficult for a child who's been reading well since she was four, but can't write well. She may be expected to pull her writing level up to her reading level. What may happen is that she struggles with the writing, but can't get it right because her reading is so advanced. As a result she becomes unhappy at school, her all-round progress suffers – and nobody knows why.

Children should be encouraged, not pressured, to write as clearly and carefully as they can, so that they can see the words they know – in their own writing. When they make mistakes, they know about them, and can work with their parents to correct them. Let the child rub out the wrongly spelled word and put in the right spelling. It will give her a lot of satisfaction. Teachers sometimes insist on crossing-outs being kept in for inspection, and teach the children to cross-out in an approved manner. But for keen children, it's just a mark of shame to keep their mistakes on view, and this method doesn't encourage pride in a neat page.

There's been a great feeling for 'creative' writing in schools over the last few years, possibly at the expense of spelling and expression. However, there may be a way out of the dilemma of whether you should inhibit your child's thoughts by insisting on correct English, or let her slap down anything to promote her creativity. Children can speak out-loud to a listener or use a tape-recorder for their wildest fantasies, then, like any other craftsman, they can use their skills at writing to get it down on paper. It would also help children to become aware of the differences between spoken and written language.

Some children have particularly strong visual awareness which helps them in reading and writing, others have to set out consciously to learn the rules like spelling and how word parts fit together. The wider the child's experience of hearing speech and playing with writing materials, the more capable he will be of tackling the complexities of English spelling.

Handwriting skills

Schools have been taking an easier attitude to handwriting skills as many of the traditional uses, such as for letter writing and clerking, have been taken over by typewriters and computers. Beautiful writing is no longer the valuable adult skill it once was. Clever children soon pick up this feeling that handwriting is no longer so important and, particularly as it can be a slow and tedious process, their enthusiasm for learning it may be lacking.

Handwriting involves not only the fingers that hold the pencil, but the whole body. A child needs a comfortable, relaxed but supported position for writing. To begin with he needs a table and chair of a suitable height; later on he will be able to write on different surfaces at different heights and under different conditions.

During writing the hand and arm should be capable of free movement and the pencil held in the correct way. Right- and left-handed children have different needs. The right-handed child should place his paper parallel to the edge of the table or at a slight angle. The left-handed child places his paper on the left and at an angle of about 45°. He also needs to hold his pencil further away from the point than the right-handed child, so that he does not cover what he's writing with his hand.

There are two important skills a child needs for writing:

Copying skill
It's difficult for a very young child to focus on individual letters and write them down in the right order to form a word or sentence, so you can ask the child to write over or trace words you have written for him. The child can then progress on to copying underneath your writing, and later on he can copy on another page. The further away his writing is from yours the harder he has to work at remembering what he's seen and the order of the letters. Bigger chunks of writing to copy mean that he has to develop the skill of finding the right place on the page in order to go on to copy the next letter or word.

Pencil control and letter formation
When a child learns to form letters correctly he is also learning to recognize them more easily in his reading – bad

writing habits lead to confusion in reading. For example, the letters 'b' and 'd' are often confused by children. This can happen if they're taught to draw a circle first and then add a stick to the left-hand side for 'b' and right-hand side for 'd'. But if they start with the stick for 'b' and the circle for 'd' they learn to form quite different letters more easily.

There are some very controversial aspects of writing, such as punctuation, creativity and the use of typewriters, which teachers often feel strongly about. Children usually show when they're ready to learn punctuation. Their writing becomes more fluent and the word 'and' is used over and over again to join up sentences. Now's the time to bring in full stops and capital letters. Clever children soon get the idea of pauses and commas. If the child is unconvinced that punctuation works, read his piece back to him without it. But patience and praise are the mainstays of improving punctuation. Don't spoil a child's work with your own comments or marks – sometimes turning a blind eye to mistakes can be more encouraging. Very early mistakes such as no spacing between words or mirror-writing normally correct themselves. Help the child to find his own errors.

The trend in teaching children to write has recently been to encourage them to write using their imagination, interests and experiences – to be creative. This is a vital and welcome change from the drudgery of hours of copying that children used to undergo. But don't expect too much, not every child is a creative genius or has a free-flowing mind; most children's work is pretty humdrum, even that of clever children.

Some clever children do have very fertile imaginations and are so keen to get a story down that their child's hand-writing skills are an encumbrance. They may feel that by the time they have painstakingly formed the letters in a legible way, they have lost the excitement, and perhaps it's not worth the trouble. A typewriter can help a lot.

Even little children can learn to type quite quickly and, once they have mastered it, it can be a handy skill for life. It can be a very much quicker way for a speedy five-year-old thinker to commit his thoughts to paper than handwriting. Critics feel that this will ruin the formation of a beautiful script, but on the other hand, creative thinking abilities are surely at least as important in the long run. Children's typewriters can be bought quite cheaply. In later years, a child's teacher can be very appreciative of typed essays to mark, rather than scruffy hand-written ones.

What you can do – writing

1. Let the baby 'draw' on thick paper with a pencil or crayon, or on a blackboard with chalks.
2. Help guide his hand around shapes as he gets older.
3. Get him to practise drawing a straight line.
4. Start him on simple jigsaws.
5. Leave him alone to draw, if he's absorbed.
6. Ask him what he's just looked at in a simple picture.
7. Find toys or objects which he can sort into sets – say by colour – as he explains what he's doing. 'This is a round shape – it's a circle – it's red' etc.
8. Play 'Join the dots' games.
9. Get him to run toy cars along painted tracks.
10. The 'Noughts and crosses' game can help.
11. Tracing patterns gives practice in moving both eye and hand from left to right, up and down, in upward and downward curves and through right angles. After a while the tracing paper can be removed and the child asked to copy simple shapes, such as:

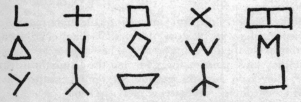

This can be done first with matches, then by moving on to drawing them.

12 Draw simple shapes with a bit missing and ask your child to fill them in, like these:

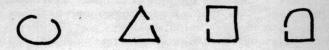

13 Ask the child to copy repetitive patterns like these:

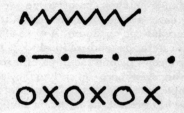

14 Always have thick, soft pencils or crayons handy.
15 Use very thin (maybe home-made) exercise books so that the child can complete them quickly and get more satisfaction.

Arithmetic

In the last ten years, new ideas have taken the teaching of numbers by storm. Most of the 'sums' that parents used to do as children have gone into disuse, while the 'new maths' has taken the focus off numbers and put it on to logical relationships and mathematical language. So instead of doing 'sums', children now measure rooms and desks and compare what they've discovered.

Parents and teachers, caught up in this whirlwind, are sometimes quite bewildered by the new maths; and why not teach tables anyway? All sorts of 'educational' teaching toys and equipment have come on to the market, and it's often difficult to tell if they're worth the expense.

Where do you start?

Babies start to learn numbers by listening to parents counting things, such as fingers or steps, over and over again. Many nursery rhymes have counting in them and clever children love these. Soon, they can write some numbers as they say them; parents should encourage this.

The language of mathematics emerges quite naturally in a lively home. For example, every time you say 'more than' or 'less than' you are teaching. Parents can bargain with children saying things such as: 'You eat up two more spoonfuls of dinner and you can have one sweet'. There's no need to force early arithmetical understanding though, it's all there in everyday conversations. A word of warning here – since children can tackle mathematical ideas without under-standing the concepts behind them, parents sometimes think their children are even more clever than they are.

Even a simple sum requires quite a lot of consideration. Firstly, a child has to understand the meaning of adding-up. Secondly, he has to be able to carry it out mentally. Thirdly, he has to cope with symbolic notation of + and = , and fourthly, he has to understand the often confusing wording of 2 and 2 are 4. So you have to try to help him in each of these four steps.

What really matters, right from the beginning, is the child's mental approach to arithmetic. It should be seen as a pleasant thing to do – really fun, and not too difficult. So many parents give children the message that maths is hard – especially for girls – that they learn to be frightened of numbers. Clever children have a real capacity to enjoy exercising their mental ability; they like doing sums and feeling good about it, even before they fully understand what they're doing. What puts children off, though, is the daily grind of sums.

Keep your touch light. Bring in as much variety as you can think of – different coloured cut-out numbers, paper with different sized squares, different kinds of things to count and move around. Think up practical exercises to do, like seeing how much water from one jar fills up another or how many beans you can put in a pot.

Little children need lots of practice at comparing sizes and shapes. The best way of starting is to get children to measure with parts of their bodies, such as the number of hand-spans, thumb-widths or foot-lengths that anything is. This provides both mental and physical gymnastics. As soon as they want to, they can move on to rulers, measuring tapes etc. Then, they make a diagram of what they've found, and make simple block graphs which can be coloured. It gives a child great satisfaction to see his work pinned up on the wall.

Weighing things is a bit more complicated. Children have to get the idea of weight and balance first. For this, they need practice at feeling the heaviness of things, and then weighing them to compare them more accurately. Start by using some simple scales to get first the idea of heavier and lighter, and then the idea of balance. When a child seems to understand these concepts, you can move on to a spring balance to see how weights are measured on a linear scale. Even clever children, though, are usually well into school before they understand about standardized weights.

The 'discovery' method

One problem with the new approach to maths was that teachers sometimes took the ideas too literally. This brought about some failures in using it. The idea of discovery was that children should learn for themselves, by handling materials and tackling practical problems. In this way they should be using their own brains, rather than being told by adults exactly what to do. What sometimes happened was that children were given a lot of teaching equipment and simply told: 'Go on, discover!'

It doesn't work. A child can't grasp the basics of maths – which it took great thinkers centuries to work out – all by himself in the maths lesson. Children need guidance and help in reading those ideas. But this doesn't mean telling them exactly what to do, nor does it mean closing the door on exploration. Teaching maths is a two-way process between teacher and child, and there has to be flexibility on both sides.

A fine example of flexibility was shown by a teacher who had an argument with a child who insisted that a triangle only had two sides. First of all, she tried to correct the child' by telling him that a triangle has three sides. 'But,' he replied, 'it has two sides and a bottom.' 'Quite right,' she agreed; after all, why should we assume that children can perceive geometrical objects as floating in Euclidian space. Obviously, children see triangles as standing up, and if so, perhaps edge is a better word to use than side.

Child mathematicians

There are a few brilliant children who are quite fluent at number work by the time they reach school. But like the early reader, these children have problems, firstly in being believed and secondly in fitting in with the level of the rest of the class. For example, an eight-year-old mathematician might have to sit through a long, laboured explanation about prime factors when he'd discovered them for himself a year or two ago. What is he to do during the lesson?

Bertrand Russell, the philosopher and mathematician, once wrote: 'At the age of eleven I began Euclid with my brother as tutor. This was one of the great events of my life, as dazzling as first love. I had not imagined there was anything so delicious in the world.'

Mathematical children can be of any personality or sex, but they all love numbers. Some have very strong feelings about their 'own' special numbers such as 7 or 3. They can add, subtract, multiply and divide in their heads from an early age, so later on when the teacher obliges them to do it in his way, stage by stage, they can get confused at having to remember it all. It's like doing P.E. with crutches.

Watch out for thinking questions from your child. 'What happens if we put 3 instead of 6?' or 'What happens if we turn the figure upside down?' or 'Let's use letters instead of' numbers.' Such children don't usually wait to be taught how to work things out; they search out problems and answers for themselves. But a problem to the ordinary child may be obviously simple to the mathematically clever one. The most valuable intellectual need for such a child is a good stock of problems which will challenge him; there are quite a number of 'problem' books in libraries and bookshops. As he gets older the child can make use of old 'O' level papers and Open University texts and perhaps his teacher can arrange for him to sit in with an older group for maths.

There is an International Olympiad for young mathematicians which is now in its twenty-fourth year. You can get information about it from the Mathematical Association. Although Russia has special schools for the mathematically gifted, there are none in Britain as yet. As a nation we don't seem to go in for that kind of hot-house treatment of children, but we haven't had any reliable evidence to show they're really beneficial to their pupils.

What to do – arithmetic

1   Encourage the baby to play with water. Start with the bathwater, to get the idea of floating, sinking, filling up cups and so on. Later on you can use ice cubes or colour the water to encourage ideas of amounts and space.

2   Let the child play with flour and water dough, squidging it through his fingers making shapes, dividing it up and so on, getting a feeling of quantity.

3   Have a sandpit if you can with cups in it. Even a small amount of sand on a big tray is sufficient, placed where it doesn't matter if it spills.

4   Toy bricks provide one of the longest lasting and most valuable toys for learning arithmetic. You will need at least sixty. They should be in proportion to each other so they fit together smoothly and look and feel nice. Different colours on the sides of the bricks add a lot to the fun of learning.

5   Fitting toys like post-boxes or nesting-dolls give practice in hand and eye coordination. This goes for jigsaw puzzles and other toys which are designed to match up.

6   Some toys hook together to make longer or shorter lines (eg toy trains), some can be threaded together (eg cotton reels), and some can be stacked on to an upright stick (eg plastic hoops).

7   Sorting-out games like miniature cars or farm animals help children to classify.

8   Give children different shapes to feel; talk about how shape affects balance and working, and how they feel about what it looks like.

9   Play shop, buying and selling food or material, for example; make pretend money, or use things like tiddly-winks for it.

10   Play dice-throwing games like snakes and ladders or ludo, especially ones that involve counting.

11   See that the child's measuring devices, such as balances and weights, are accurate.

Chapter 6

EARLY SUCCESS AT SCHOOL

All the good preparation which parents put into their children's early lives goes to work when their child comes under the care of a teacher. For many children this can start from about the age of two, when they may begin with a few hours a week at nursery school.

Though there are parents who do not like the idea of such little children being away from their homes regularly, perhaps even daily, there is quite a lot of evidence to show that children who go to nursery school settle down more quickly and get on better at infant school. My own four children all went to a nursery school starting in their third year. It seemed to me, as a mother, that they were all very happy there and none of them had problems in transferring to 'proper' school.

What a nursery school can do

When a child is about three he begins to need a bit of social life. His nearest and dearest, on whom he has been dependent for so long, somehow do not quite fill his life completely any more and parents may well need a break too. One way of helping a child's social life along, now and in the future, is to give him the company of others his own age. It helps a little child to get a sense of identity and encourages his unfolding individuality.

The exclusive parent-child relationship, which has endured all his life so far, is not 'natural' in many societies – it only happens in the Western world. All over Africa and China, for instance, parents have children playing with other children as soon as they can stagger about. There's no convincing psychological or anthropological evidence to suggest that parenting is instinctive or even natural; we behave as parents in the way we're taught to behave. If children are only supplied with the love and care of their parents and prevented from getting to know others of their own age, even as toddlers, they lose an essential dimension of early experience – other children – and social learning. When children don't go to nursery school, parents should be careful to see that they still have plenty of opportunities to get to know other children.

It has long been a part of common knowledge that toddlers, from about two-and-a-half years old, can take comfort in being with others of their own age and older children as well. In a famous experiment, the American Professor Harry Harlow[1] showed that young monkeys raised with food but without their mothers were not able to grow up to lead normal social lives. But when he allowed them to be with their age-mates, for as little as twenty minutes a day, their social, intellectual and emotional development was much less retarded than that of others who had been totally isolated from friends. Studies with human infants have found that a child's valuable source of language learning can be other children at nursery school. Even so, the child's fullest linguistic capacities are still best developed from talk at home, which can be richer and more finely tuned than most of the interactions at nursery school.

Unfortunately, there are not enough state nursery schools in Britain for all the parents who would like to use them. Many are private and, though excellent, are expensive. Others have opening hours which make it difficult for working parents to leave their children there. The French have made a big effort to extend nursery school hours which has been very successful and this could be done here for comparatively little money and with great benefit to the children. Another idea is to use classrooms, which are now becoming available with the decline in the school population, to house nursery classes.

Another way in which children can get together is in a

playgroup. These came about as a sort of 'do it yourself' cooperative nursery school during the 1960s and have now become the nationwide Preschool Playgroups Association. You can track down your local one in your telephone directory. The playgroups are not run on identical lines and tend to focus more on play and learning to socialize than instruction for the children. One problem for working parents in using playgroups is that they are expected to take their share of running the group, which may not always fit in with the work schedule.

But without either of these facilities, working parents are often obliged to use the services of grandparents willing to help out or a paid preschool child minder, who may or may not be registered. Although possibly quite acceptable as minders, in terms of early education an untrained child minder is no substitute for a nursery teacher. Quite a number of recent surveys into child minding, including the one by the TUC[2], have provided reason for some concern. For example Professor Jerome Bruner, an educationalist concerned with care of the under-fives in Britain, found from his Oxford survey that childminding 'is a risky form of care even with sympathetic and kindly, conventionally competent child minders'[3]. Obviously every childminder should be judged on her own merits, as such statements are only very general. Bruner suggested that childminders would be most suitably employed working alongside trained child care givers. They could be used as extras in nursery schools, or as a timely help between the close of school and parents finishing work.

All pre-school education, whether playgroup or nursery school, is an extension, not a substitute, for the private family world in which children grow best. The progression from home to pre-school should be as smooth and easy as possible. Parents should never feel that they are giving over control of their child's early education to a nursery school teacher. The family is still all-important. For all that he is away a few hours a day, the child is still a member of his

133

family and his parents are still the most influential people he knows.

What to look for in a nursery school

1   Is the atmosphere lively and are the children's educational experiences stimulating?
2   Are the staff well trained and do they stay?
3   Is the nursery well organized or is there little rationale in the activities chosen?
4   Is there a warm and loving atmosphere?
5   Is the atmosphere designed to make children feel at ease and happy? A nursery is not a copy of home, but it can have an intimate feeling by, for example, having the children in little groups for special play or listening to a story. It should be like a child's second home.
6   Do the staff and children seem to get on together, or is there a feeling that the children have to do as they're told – or else? That punitive atmosphere can make children unhappy and set up anti-education feelings in them for life.

Working along with teacher

Few teachers will find themselves with a Mozart or an Einstein in their class, but they will all be in charge of clever children at some time – and one of these may be yours. Parents can help their children to do their best at school when they understand what the teachers are trying to do, and by working along with them. This can begin when your child has just started nursery school, and it goes right on till the end of secondary school in much the same way.

It sometimes happens that parents and teacher may not agree on the cleverness of the child – one man's geese are another man's swans – and children may not behave the same way at school as at home. For example, a clever little boy who is thriving and into everything at home may try to fit in with what he thinks is wanted of him at school, to please the teacher. So he may cut down on asking the questions that come to his mind, or do his homework exactly as he thinks is required – and no more – though he's really capable of much more imaginative and interesting work. In this way, parents and teacher are both justified in seeing quite different pictures of the boy.

A six-year-old was heard by his mother reading aloud in a flat, uninteresting style to himself, though he had often read with life and enthusiasm to her. 'Why are you doing that?' she asked. 'When I do that at school,' he replied, 'teacher says "very good".'

Appearance counts too. When the teacher sees her pupil clean, tidy and ready to work, she's more likely to see him as clever than the one who's a mess and doesn't seem to care about school. She's also more likely to treat him more favourably, without even being aware of it herself. Although parents may not care much about their child's appearance themselves, it's a good idea to send your child to school looking ready for school work. My bright teenage daughter often questioned this idea, with reason: 'How does wearing a ring to school affect my ability to learn?' It doesn't, of course, but it does affect the teacher.

Teachers' ideas of who is clever and who isn't are very often influenced by the type of children who go to the school. In some areas, where parents are able to do a lot to help their children, the teacher may describe children as clever only when they do very well in tests and exams. As a result, some clever children, who are not the best in that particular school, may be under-rated. The opposite can happen in a school which draws children from culturally poor homes; teachers may feel that no-one clever could come from such surroundings. Once, when I was researching for clever children, a headteacher said to me: 'You'll not find any clever ones in my school – they're all council house children.' She then refused me permission to find out for myself by going in to see the children. Parents have to work extra hard for their clever children if they have to go to a school where the headteacher has that kind of attitude.

The teachers' reactions to the child's culture can sometimes hamper his school progress. If, for example, a working-class boy was to use language which came naturally to him in a school essay, the teacher might find it grammatically incorrect and mark him down. When any child, however clever, constantly sees his spontaneous thoughts and ideas crossed out in red he may lose heart. Children with culturally different backgrounds need special care and encouragement from parents and teachers. The boyhood of Emlyn Williams, portrayed so beautifully in his book *The Corn is Green*, shows how an educationally disadvantaged boy can be helped to success by a kind and interested teacher.

It can happen that a clever child may find herself working below her ability, in a lower stream of a rigidly organized school. This used to happen quite frequently when clever children were misplaced by the eleven-plus exam, which made mistakes in about ten per cent of all its selections. Thousands of clever children who should have gone to grammar schools were sent to unacademic secondary modern schools, where they began to think of themselves as failures and stopped exercising their intellectual abilities, although they would have been quite capable of going to university.

Some writers such as Ivan Illich, who wrote *Deschooling Society*, believe that schools are organizations devoted to making new citizens conform to society's rules. Others say that schools have almost no effect, and that everything which helps a child to get on in the world comes from the home. But recent research by Professor Michael Rutter in London[2] has found that schools do have some effect on children – after all, they spend a lot of their time there, and schools have individual outlooks and practices which can be measured.

The way children feel about themselves and their abilities can have a marked influence on how they get on at school. They're not only sensitive to the way the teacher sees them, but also to their schoolmates' opinions. Sometimes, exceptionally clever children may feel that they are looked on as odd, even in very academic schools, so they may hide their clever-

136

ness a little to seem more normal and make more friends. Parents should watch out for this (which is discussed further on page 155) and give the child lots of support and love, so that he can feel confident enough to shine in his own way – and still make friends. It's strange how this situation only applies to children who are intellectually clever – brilliant athletes only ever seem to receive praise. Fortunately, as children get older, they usually become more accurate in judging how well they can do at school, if they want to. For those who are lucky enough to have parents who really care, it's possible to get on with the job of being successful at school.

The will to learn

The cornerstone of good learning is the will to learn – motivation. Many clever children are not motivated to learn, either at home or at school, and when they have fallen into a pattern of not achieving as much as they could, it's not likely to right itself naturally. Parents have to step in.

If a child is to do well, he must want to do well. The saying has it that you can take a horse to water, but you can't make it drink. In educational terms you can provide your child with all the intellectual nourishment anyone could want – like good quality toys, the finest schools, and a lovely home, but you can't make him want to be successful. How does it happen, then, that some children are motivated to do well and some aren't?

Motivation is the result of a child coming to expect things, because of what he does. A two-year-old, for example, can reasonably expect to build a pile of six bricks. He's not sure at first, of course, but when he does succeed he's most gratified, and may be spurred on to try seven bricks next time. But if he fails, his estimate of what he can do may take a tiny knock. Depending on the way he feels about it, he may try again and fail – causing another tiny knock – or succeed, and feel better about himself. He may fail because the bricks are not as well made as the last set he played with, but then his expectations would not be founded on a real situation. Or he may fail because he's over-reached himself. Either way, his expectations and hopes for his next tower-block may become a little lower, as a result of his experience on this one.

In this trial-and-error way, a child comes to judge what he can do, and when he might be able to do it. He'll use parents' and teachers' judgements a lot in helping to form his guidelines. For a child to do his best, you should encourage him to aim a bit higher next time, but his expectations should not be too high or too low – the judgement is a delicate one.

When parents expect too much of their child, so that he's bound to fail often, he can lose confidence in his own judgement and become more and more dependent on their ideas of what he can do. He may also see himself as a growing failure. Children who are recognized as clever are in special danger of this happening to them. For example, parents may expect clever children to be successful in *everything* they do. But children, like adults, have their ups and downs, and are better at some things than others.

Children can be taught to feel sure of what they can do, and so helped towards wanting to do their best. Both motivation to do well and independence of thought stem from feelings of security and support, which are learned very early in life. This means giving the child a feeling of pride in the things that he does well, so that he can be sure that his parents' praise and attention will follow whenever he tries to do well.

Parents play a very important part in a child's will to learn and succeed. Those who see their children as independent little people right from the start, allow them freer expression and are less critical, are more likely to have children who achieve well. Children of parents who use a lot of control, are over-protective and unwilling to reason with them generally do less well.

Many people who have eventually become eminent and

who must have been clever children, didn't always do well at school – Einstein for one, Churchill for another. But once they were motivated, there was no stopping them. A study of 400 prominent figures[3] showed that, although they loved learning, three out of five were poor performers at school. If children seem to be failing at specific tasks, try to help them tackle their problems with new approaches. Get them to ask 'How can I do this?' instead of 'Can I do this?'

When clever children don't want to learn, there are usually good reasons for it. Sometimes it is due to emotional problems, but very often there are more straightforward difficulties, such as these below, stemming from the approach of parents and teachers to the business of learning.

Meaning

Where a child has more than one teacher – which is usually the case – some teaching may not seem to have any connection with the rest. What may happen is that the thinking skills which a child learns with one teacher don't seem to apply to another teacher's lessons. To the child, it may also seem that school learning doesn't connect up with 'real' life anyway, so the whole thing becomes a pointless exercise. As tedious lesson exercises are fortunately being used very much less, and teachers are getting together more in their approaches to children, this handicapping of a child's feeling for learning should also get less. Learning has to be meaningful to the child, so if you have to, point the meanings out. Take children to places where they can see what's taught at school put into use. The most obvious connection is probably sums and money; don't do all the paying for the shopping yourself – let the child do it and make sure it's correct. Let him help with weighing for cooking and measuring for the new floor covering for example.

Tests

Some schools are very fond of weekly tests and giving marks. Clever children can find these irritating, because they know how inadequate the tests are, and often what a waste of time too. To some extent, teachers have to give tests to find out how different members of the class are getting on, but they can also be used to increase a clever child's motivation. Rather than just asking for facts to be reproduced, tests can be creative, using the child's thinking skills and imagination. They can measure decision-making and judgement, which is much more interesting for a clever child. Clever children can get bored with ordinary tests and, if so, they may show up poorly in them. If you think this may be a problem, talk about it with the teacher.

Difficulty

More than most others, clever children get into the position where the learning is either too easy or too difficult for them. They have to proceed at their own rate, either skipping some stages that other children need to complete, or finding a challenge that they cannot meet. A teacher can easily over-estimate the ability of a clever child, who may find the work too difficult at that time and give up trying. This can be a problem for clever children who are moved up and miss out a class. Parents may have to point this out to teachers – in the nicest possible way. Don't be too ambitious for your child; though she may be very clever, she may be happier and learn better in a steady, less challenging class. You don't have to agree when the school suggests she jump a year, if you don't think it's right for your child.

Correction

You can correct a clever child too minutely. Who wants to give his 'all' in a story, only to be constantly corrected for small mistakes? Clever children have to explore ideas, rather than record known facts. They're much keener to learn when there's an element of exploration in their learning. Really listen to a child's early reading, for example. Your genuine enthusiasm for his stumbling success is much more encouraging than putting him right.

A child can either learn in fits and starts or make smooth progress; it depends on what's being learned and on how it's taught. For instance, if you're trying to teach a toddler how to read, but the baby keeps interrupting, he won't remember his learning as well as if he had no interruptions. But if he has some reading practice just before going to sleep, so that there's a long time without disturbance, his learning 'takes hold' better. Parents can help their children to good learning, both at home and in school, by using the following suggestions.

Encourage the will to learn

All children start off by wanting to learn. If this will seems to be lacking, parents should try to find the cause, and help their child over it. Check on matters such as feeling unhappy with a teacher, friends not being nice, or insecurity at home, which can all affect a child's willingness to learn. Check on the way the school is teaching – has your child any special problems with the methods it uses?

Try to get your child's progress into perspective. Sometimes parents, who are so closely involved, become worried over what they feel is poor learning, though the child may really be doing very well. When our first child was barely toddling, for example, my husband and I were very concerned about his slow progress in talking, as we saw it. So, one day we put our heads together and counted all the words he could say. They totalled fifty – quite a lot really – and we never worried about his talking again.

Rewards

Rewards can be a very effective way to encourage children to learn. Parents who think positively, who use praise lavishly (where it's justified), and who give treats (small) for extra effort will probably have a child who feels happy about learning. Sarcasm and punishment are very much less effective in helping children to learn. A child may be misbehaving and doing badly at school to get extra attention. In that case, punishment may fit his emotional bill, but won't improve his learning.

Feedback

Good feedback from work done well is warmly satisfying. It also helps a child to set his sights at the right level; he can then avoid both certain failure from work that's too hard, and too quick success from work that's too easy.

Both success and failure in learning tend to perpetuate themselves. Parents can alter the feedback to allow a child a feeling of success, and so positively enhance his will to learn more. Take a simple example of a toddler learning to carry a cup of water without spilling it. If the cup is too full for him to manage at his age, he'll get negative feedback, in the form of water on the floor and of parental dismay in his ears, and may feel 'put down'. When the water's at a level he can manage, and the job is carried out to perfection, he'll feel good about it and receive the praise due to him. A child draws conclusions from each learning experience, so that his approach to new learning depends very much on what's gone before.

Family feeling
All families exert a certain amount of influence on their members, and much of it is in the form of example by the parents. When parents are active and keenly interested in life around them, then the likelihood is that their children will be the same. Show your children, by your example, that learning gives a lifetime of pleasure, and that as a way of life it's worth following. Take part in learning about things along with your children, so that they don't feel learning is only something for children, to be forgotten when they grow up.

Flexible learning
The best kind of learning is flexible, so that the lessons learned in one situation can be applied in another. It's something that clever children are particularly good at. One clever little girl, who learned that water expands on freezing, froze some water in a plastic bottle to stretch it – and it worked.

Old learning can get in the way of new learning, when it's not appropriate. When children change schools, for example, and have to learn another method of long division, they'll take longer over this than they did with the first method. Old learning which becomes really entrenched is called 'habit', and becomes more and more difficult to shift as it becomes embedded.

Action

Everyone has to take an active part in their own learning, whether by sand and water play, by talking about things, or by mixing chemicals. The least efficient way of learning anything is to listen to someone else telling you about it – like a lecture. Whenever you can, think of ways in which your child can learn by doing something. For example, don't describe an electrical circuit to your son, but set one up together with him.

Young children have to learn that when they put more effort into learning, they are more likely to be successful; older children can see more easily that they have to work to learn well. It's no use, therefore, insisting to little children that they have to try harder at school to bring up their standard of, say, writing. The understanding will come of its own accord, to some extent, though gentle encouragement is always welcome.

As clever children get older, they usually become attracted to more complicated pieces of learning, like maths problems which they can really get their teeth into. They sometimes use less clever children as markers, whom they feel they should pass. It adds a little 'spice' to the very enjoyable activity of learning.

Good study methods

Learning how to learn begins when a clever child is tiny, yet it can affect the way she will tackle any task throughout her life. This may be right at the beginning when she finds out that skill and patience are more likely to get her shaped block through the slot in the toy 'post box' than banging it down angrily; and she'll use that understanding again. Later on she may find that she has better friendships if she doesn't grab toys from her mates' hands at nursery school. Soon she will learn how to get the teacher's attention by asking for it in just the right way: children who are too shy are sometimes left alone by the teacher and so can miss some vital teaching, whereas those who are too demanding may be pushed aside in irritation at their behaviour.

In writing about study methods here, I'm concerned with a child's growing mastery of his own learning, but these acquired skills can also be very useful for older children and parents. Though you are probably reading this book to find out more about clever children, perhaps it may offer a bonus!

Having the right approach to their work from their first days at school can make a big difference to children's learning, which shows when they come to the tests and exams later. Good study habits formed at home and at school also continue to be of great value as youngsters move on from school to higher education and adult life. But schools don't usually teach study methods, which is really a little strange, so most children usually have to struggle through on their own. Yet the basis of good study is easily remembered by a clever child, and can offer him great satisfaction in practice. Here are some ideas which can be useful throughout childhood:

The will to study

Again, the question of motivation is foremost here, and problems with it are not uncommon. Clever children often become devoted to just a few aspects of their interests – say, science and not the arts at school – so that they won't sit down and learn history, as they're supposed to. Find out why this is so; talk about it with the child. Sometimes a subject can be dropped with no harm done, but it may need to be gone through, even mechanically, just to provide a reasonably wide educational base. The child should understand why he is expected to do this particular work, though; there has to be something in it for him too, not just for parents or for the sake of school routine. Even infant-level clever children can understand that learning about other people (geography and history) helps them to learn about the world, so that they can cope with their own lives a little better, that English helps them to communicate and sums means they pay the correct price.

Organization

Parents often work on the assumption that teachers are helping children to develop study skills at home, but this is most often not so. There is, of course, set homework, but clever children may want to work around that or follow their own interests. Any investigation is more effective when it is properly organized. Firstly, it is usually best to take an overall view of what is to be done, whether project or exam revision. The child should learn to plan out her intended programme and then to fill in the detail to be covered, preferably so that the mind does not have to waste energy in drastic refocussing from one style of thought to another. For example, a secondary school child could arrange to revise chemistry followed by physics, then biology, geography, history and so on.

Physical surroundings

There are two schools of thought about noise when studying. Some say there shouldn't be any, but others find relief in quiet constant background noise, such as the hum of distant traffic or quiet music. Many, such as my teenage children, say that they like to study to loud music, but I remain sceptical as to whether they're doing their best work at such times.

A heavy meal causes blood to flow away from the brain to assist the digestive organs in their work and makes you feel sleepy; the same results come from a hot bath or drinking alcohol, with the blood supply to the brain diminishing in each case. Too comfortable a chair, too warm a room, poor light or not enough fresh air can all handicap study too.

It helps continuity when the studying can always be done in the same place so, if you can, spare a little space for your child's own study use. When a child can go to her familiar chair or desk, pick up the pencil from where she left it, and take up her ideas again from where she left off, her settling down time will be much reduced. If the study area can be organized in such a way that it only needs the arrival of the child to complete the familiar set-up, then the processes of learning will flow almost automatically.

Remembering

There are often good reasons for forgetting things, or remembering them wrongly. A child soon forgets something that he doesn't like or finds boring. Looking back, you may remember that sometimes when you'd finished the task for which you'd been learning something, as for an exam, you seemed to forget it all as you left the room. Unless you were going to use that particular learning again soon, you possibly lost it altogether then. On the other hand, an unfinished task has a sort of hangover effect – it stays on to be remembered. So, a good study habit for both young and old is to leave your work not quite finished at the end of the day. The next day, you'll find it easier to get into it again.

Reading

There are ways of reading which can speed up compre-hension so that the reader gets the author's message quickly and accurately. Tony Buzan's book *Use Your Head*[4] describes many ways of improving reading and studying. With practice, it is possible to take in greater gulps of words at a time, instead of reading each word separately. Then, instead of reading across the lines of print, you can skim a page downwards, to see what's on it. If you want to see some part of it in more detail, you can always go back for another look. Clever children are well able to start such speed-reading by the time they reach secondary school.

How to study

1   Children should skim the work to be done – purposefully – so that they have a rough idea of what is to be covered. Directed effort, with an end-product, is better than vague searching. For example, a little child can make an

effort to learn the letter 'B' rather than messing about with lots of different letters.

2   Try to relate new material to what the child knows already. For example, John's splashing in the sink has taught him a lot about water movement. Why not show him how it balances itself in both arms of a U-shaped transparent plastic tube – the beginnings of physics.

3   Learning is easier in comprehensible chunks, rather than unrelated fragments, because we remember better that way. Get Mary to read a whole story regularly, not just a little bit. Start the reading with plenty of time to spare so you aren't cut short. But longer stories, read a chapter at a time, have their valuable place too.

4   Half-understood words or passages should be looked up at the time they are read. When you think you under-stand, but you're not quite sure, it's much easier to forget what you are supposed to be learning. Junior school children soon get in the habit of looking words up in their dictionaries if they're taught to do so.

5   Get older children to write down a summary of what they're reading or have listened to – in their own words. This guarantees that they're having to think it through. Also, get them to emphasize the main points or principles in brief, so that they become really involved with it. A good idea is to write down the essential facts about any one subject on a postcard, which can be carried around.

6   Children can say what they've learned out loud, even to themselves. This soon shows the bits they're not quite clear on. Children often do this quite naturally unless they're made to feel embarrassed about talking to them-selves.

7   Mnemonic systems can be helpful in a difficult situation, where there are unrelated lists to be remembered. We use one for the music scale, for example – Good Boys Deserve Fruit – though many music teachers believe that this type of rote learning may hinder a deeper musical appreciation.

Can school success be predicted?

The problem in trying to predict how well your child will do at school is that between a child's ability to do well and the fulfilment of his potential, there's a whole world of 'ifs' and 'buts'. It's extremely difficult to predict the development of an ability that hasn't yet had a chance to be tried out. For instance, Van Gogh, the painter, didn't have the opportunity to start painting until he was an adult; it's doubtful whether anyone could have predicted his artistic success when he was a child, and in fact, because of his innovatory style, he was never widely acknowledged as a 'proper' painter in his own lifetime.

Not all schools teach the same subjects or develop the same interests in children, even at primary level. I have visited a junior school, for example, where there wasn't a single musical instrument in the building. Yet not far away, there was a very similar school that had over thirty children learning the guitar. The difference was that none of the teachers in the first school were interested in music, but the second school had an enthusiastic man on the staff, who wanted to share his joy in the guitar with his pupils. Needless to say, there were no talented child musicians in the first school.

Parents and teachers can only guess at future success from the way the child is seen to behave at the time. For example, there must be millions of boy babies who have had boxing or footballing careers predicted for them in their first few weeks of life. Sometimes parents really would like their children to grow up in a certain way, so they look for – and find – signs of it while the children are quite small. In this way a girl can reach the age of, say, ten, 'knowing' that she's going to be a nurse. Well, she did bandage her doll's leg, and she did stick a plaster on her brother's finger. And for many children, the predictions come true because they're not given much encouragement to consider doing anything else.

The best way of predicting future success at anything is to see how well a child can do it at present and how keen he is to go on with it. The key lies in the child's own feelings about wanting success in that area. The five-year-old who loves playing with dough may not turn out to be a baker, but he may find so much satisfaction in handling shapes that he ends up as a sculptor.

There are psychological tests which are used to predict success for children. These are based on accumulated evidence from the way abilities have developed in many thousands of children. From his result in the test a child can be compared with all this past evidence. But it doesn't always work. Every child is unique and has his own pattern of development, so that he may not fulfil the expectation calculated for him on the basis of all the other children's results.

Intelligence tests are made up in the same way, based on thousands of other children's developmental patterns. (See Chapter 3 for more about IQ.) They're very good predictors of success for groups of children, such as a school class, but can sometimes be wrong for any one child. For example, many children with only moderate IQs may not do well at school, but become successful afterwards. Maurice Sendak, the writer and illustrator of children's books, was like that – a bright intelligent boy, but no scholar. He left school and worked at a number of jobs until he found that what he really wanted to do was write and illustrate children's stories. It was something he had always enjoyed doing and he was brilliant at it, even if the school didn't appreciate his talents. Now he's a millionaire.

No matter how good the test, a child's results in it can be affected by what is happening on the day he takes it. They can also be affected by how he feels about taking tests – scared or excited; how he thinks his teacher feels about him – loving or disapproving; whether he's feeling well or is harbouring a cold, and so on.

So test results for the same child can vary from day to day, but they can also vary through life. A child's IQ, for instance, can change a lot over a few years, depending on his circumstances. Sometimes where a child's intellectual growth has been held back, for reasons such as extreme poverty, he can catch up when life takes a turn for the better.

Success in school is very often measured by the child's obvious achievement there, such as passing exams. But there's so much more that's learned in school – like how to learn or think critically, and attitudes or values which perhaps can't be seen till much later in life. Clever children may find memorizing facts for exams an irksome task, whereas discussion is much more stimulating for them. Consequently, they may give their teachers a false picture of their real potential, unless they have the kind of teachers and parents who look beyond exam success. Predictions for individuals are always something of a 'guestimate', whether from the most complicated statistical calculations, or from the most sensitive interpretations of a child's behaviour.

What you can do – for success in school

1   If you put a high value on education then your children probably will too.

2   Try to see that your child has all he needs to work with and learn from, like plenty of paper and pencils and a corner of his own.

3   If your child enjoys peace of mind he's likely to learn more easily and do better at school.

4   If you feel your child is ready for it, try to find him a good nursery school. If there isn't one nearby, find out about pre-school playgroups from your nearest Pre-School Playgroups Association – they provide very valuable experiences for toddlers. Look for this in your local telephone directory.

5   Work along with your child's teacher for the best results for your child. If you think the teacher really hasn't got his measure, talk to her about your worries first. Teaching a child yourself, in contradiction to what he's learning at school, can be confusing to him.

6   Home emotional support is invaluable to a clever child

who wants to do her best, especially if the rest of the class disapproves of a pupil who works too hard.

7 Try to keep your expectations for your child in line with what he's capable of doing. The art is in getting him to exert himself without placing the goal so high that he's bound to fail in the attempt. Don't, for example, jump a reading book because you think you've got a clever child. Though he may be reading fluently, he may still need to take each step as it comes.

8 It can be hard to do, but try to keep up your child's interest in what he is supposed to be learning. Nothing kills off the will to learn more quickly than boredom. Learning has to seem to be relevant to the learner for it to be taken in well.

9 Allow your child to stumble in her road to learning. Watch yourself to see that you are not correcting every little error in her grammar while she's trying to tell you something.

10 Reward good learning with affection and occasionally perhaps a present, but only where the effort the child has made merits it. Reward for no real effort loses its effect.

11 Help children to learn how to learn from the beginning by following the ideas set out in this chapter.

12 Encourage children to follow their ideas through, as far as they can.

13 Show initiative and interest as parents in what your child is trying to do. Take him to museums and historical places, for example, to fill in the background to his interests. But don't overdo it; it's his interest which should guide you, not your keenness to be good parents.

Chapter 7

TOO CLEVER BY HALF

Many misguided ideas circulate about clever children. For example, you may have heard people say that the cleverer children are, the odder they are. Very clever children are expected to be undersized, bespectacled, no good at sport, miserable and lonely. But this is all a myth, for clever children are basically no different from other children except for that one thing – their cleverness. Doubtless there are some very clever children who are odd, but plenty of average children have problems too. What sometimes happens is that because clever children are expected to be a bit different, they're given some degree of licence to behave differently. So when an average four-year-old throws a temper tantrum, it's seen for what it is; but when a child who's considered to be clever throws one, it may be interpreted as an example of his supposed intellectual 'frustration', 'only to be expected'.

This idea is taken to an extreme when genius is thought of as akin to madness. Though there have been geniuses who were mentally disturbed, such as Virginia Woolf, the writer, or Van Gogh, the painter, their mental disturbances certainly weren't part of their great gifts. In fact, when they became really 'mad', it stopped their creative work entirely. One can name many more geniuses who were quite normal psychiatrically, from Leonardo da Vinci to Edison, the American inventor; genius is far more likely to call for clear thinking and hard work than craziness. Marie Curie, for example, had to melt down hundreds of tons of pitch to get at her drop of radium – the beginnings of X-rays. Her dedicated labour was both mentally and physically hard and she was, of course, perfectly sane.

There are also some ideas circulating that clever children may be somehow less moral than other children. Take some words we use daily in English to describe different forms of cleverness, but which also mean a doubtful morality or an untrustworthy person. A highly skilled person may be called 'artful' or 'crafty', for instance, or someone with swift reactions may be accused of using 'sleight of hand' or being 'sly', and intellectual cleverness is known derogatively as 'cunning' or, in the case of foreigners and uneducated people, 'native cunning'.

The following quote from a newspaper, dated 1974, brings the point about clever children's delicate morality up to date: '"Highly gifted children are in danger of becoming drop-outs and delinquents, or even super-cunning criminals, because schools are failing to give them an education that matches their abilities," headteachers said yesterday.' Fortunately this can't possibly be true, because there would be clever children plotting mayhem all over the place – though perhaps they're simply too clever to get caught! The great train robbers are sometimes described as examples of clever children who went wrong because their educations were not stimulating enough. The law, however, does not accept that clever children have these overwhelming problems which drive them to crime, and neither do I.

In the mid-1970s I began an investigation to find out (among other things) whether cleverness in children affected their behaviour with other people[1]. I wanted to see whether children labelled as exceptionally clever were any different from those of equal ability who were not spotted. Fortunately I was able to use the records of the National Association for Gifted Children. Parents join this organization if they believe their child is cleverer than the average, but no test or other form of verification is required. Of the 4500 children registered, I tested seventy from the northwest of England and found that their abilities varied from above average to truly gifted. Then I compared these parent-chosen children with children of the same intellectual ability from the same school classes, which eliminated any effects of school, district, sex or age on the children's performances. I visited all the children's homes and schools, asked a lot of questions and gave a lot of tests, and then analyzed the results.

What I found was that the children most likely to be considered exceptionally able were those who were the least well behaved at home or school. Many people believe that brilliance brings problems, but in fact this is untrue. Equally able children, who did not make nuisances of themselves, were simply less likely to be singled out as 'typically' gifted. So a child's native ability alone was unlikely to bring him to notice as a gifted child unless it was associated with problem behaviour. This fits in with the myth.

Children who are seen as 'too' clever can be treated just as oddly as is the idea of over-cleverness in the first place. Here is an example of what happened to Noel Coward, an undoubtedly clever child, from *The Life of Noel Coward* by C. Lesley (Jonathan Cape): 'When Noel was still two the doctor pronounced that his brain was much in advance of his body and advised that he should be left very quiet, that all his curls should be cut off and that he was to go to no parties.' He seems to have made up for it later, though.

You may think that this doctor's ideas belong to a past age, yet I have come across a few similar situations in my research. There was a five-year-old boy, for example, who lived with his disabled mother and who was proving very difficult for her to handle. The family doctor made it quite clear to me that it was all the mother's fault. She had, he said, overstimulated the boy with nursery rhymes and refused to take his prescription of keeping her child indoors and quiet.

There's no use trying to judge your child's cleverness by his social behaviour. There are proportionally many more average children who misbehave than clever ones, though clever ones aren't always angels either. Being clever is a matter of intellectual ability, what a child has the mental capacity to do, so if there are behaviour problems, look further for their real source (see Chapter 4).

Problems at school

Whether they receive their first outside learning from a play-group or a nursery school, children who are above average have special needs and problems of which parents and teachers should be aware and work together to solve. These problems are not always obvious when the children are very tiny, but they seem to grow as the children move further on into the school system. If they are not taken into account, they can result in a clever child not fulfilling his potential.

Some of these problems are to do with the organization and attitudes of schools and teachers. For instance very few local education authorities offer specialist help for clever children in the form of advisers or special teachers, or even a recognition of the fact that clever children have special needs at all. Fewer than half of all primary school headteachers feel that clever children need any special educational provision. In addition they are sometimes pushed aside by teachers as being 'too clever', and the idea that some children are so clever that they should have special attention seems 'elitist', as many headteachers told me in my research.

In a recent Schools Council Enquiry[2], over half the teachers who were surveyed thought that very clever children were hampered, in primary schools especially, by an anti-intellectual spirit. This means that little consideration is given to developing the extra gifts these children have, for example, by providing them with more advanced books or science equipment.

Sometimes clever children deliberately hide their capabilities when they get to school, though they rarely do at home. Teachers and parents can tell when this is happening from the fact that these children aren't doing as well as they should be, though they are very unlikely to appear at the bottom of the class. They very cunningly put themselves in the middle. That's not where they should be, and it's way below a clever child's potential standard of work. But this does make it difficult for the teacher to spot them and draw them up to their rightful place.

155

Six-year-old Belinda's teacher, for example, argued with her parents that she couldn't be as clever as they seemed to think. The teacher hadn't seen any signs of it, so his conclusions were quite justified. However, that week he caught Belinda writing a maths textbook from some basic principles she'd worked out for herself. From then on he saw what her parents meant, gave Belinda some extra attention and understanding, and soon she began to flourish.

Clever children who hide themselves among other children can seem contented in a superficial way. They enjoy television, comics and books like any other children and spend their time in play and chat with friends. They don't need a lot of time or energy to keep up with the mainstream, so they don't have to try hard at school or homework. But you know and they know that they'd be much happier and mentally livelier if they stretched themselves – in other words, if they behaved naturally. Trying to be like everyone else can be a bit of a strain.

There are times, though, when the other children in the class make it difficult for a clever child to learn at her own pace. They say she's 'teacher's pet' or a 'swot' or a 'show-off'. One clever little girl, Sally, whom I know well, was once taken out of her class to a higher one for a few minutes. When she got there, the teacher asked her to write a hard-to-spell word on the board, in front of the older children. She quickly realized that she was being used to shame the older children by showing them that a younger child could spell a word that they couldn't. 'That's a poor method of teaching,' she thought, and out of sympathy for the other pupils she knowingly spelled the word wrongly on the board. Nothing was said, and she returned to her own class, but the teacher must have got the message, since Sally wasn't asked to do it again.

Many clever children who have 'made it' in the past did so in spite of, rather than because of, the education they received at school. That's why parents are the best resource a clever child is likely to have, especially if the school doesn't seem to be coping with his special needs. Most clever children really do need some adult help to fulfil their potential. Some clever children are in schools which actually put a brake on their development, for example, by not allowing them to use advanced equipment when they're ready for it, or by leaving their curious minds unsatisfied about questions outside the school syllabus, such as ethical and moral ones. It's a kind of censorship of the mind. There are many priorities in education, but clever children have a right to be one of them. However, there's still a long way to go before their needs are both fully recognized and properly met.

Clever children in schools are usually well aware of the style and quality of the education they are receiving. Below are some comments made to me by very bright junior school children which point out, with some wry humour, aspects of their school lives which are less than helpful to them in developing their learning potential.

Brian (age eleven): 'You spend four years in junior school persuading your teacher that you're a nice boy, but work . . . no way . . . you tell jokes and show how happy you are.'

Wendy (age nine): 'If it wasn't for the ambition of the pupils, the school would collapse.'

Sarah (age nine): 'If a teacher tells you to shut up, she tells you to go to sleep. Then you wake up when the bell goes.'

Andrew (age ten): 'The teacher who screams about heads rolling is regarded as a twit. Teachers who regard themselves as respected are a pain in the neck.'

Gillian (age eleven): 'Our primary school teacher was drunk on power; he could do anything, make anyone cry. I used to count the cracks on the ceiling, and had all sorts of games I could play while he was telling me how hopeless I was.'

Kevin (age eight): 'A poor teacher, says "It's like that"; a good teacher says, "Why *is* it like that?".'

Henry (age seven): 'You don't learn when the teacher's in a bad mood; you have to learn it the next lesson, when he's in a good mood. When I sleep in lessons, my head gets itchy.

The one benefit of TV is that I don't go to sleep.'

Robert (age eleven): 'A teacher decides on your grades. If you tell good jokes and have short hair, you're OK. But even if you come top of the class and the teacher thinks you're stupid, he'll continue to believe it.'

Stephen (age eleven): 'Kids are dangerous things that mess up your school. Teachers are in competition with their classes, because there's all this competition in education.'

As Hylda Baker might have said, 'They know, you know!'

Clever children need a style of education at school that takes their special abilities into account and which can offer them greater challenges than average children could manage. This implies that their teachers should have some ideas of how to spot clever children and what to do with them, such as devising interesting and stimulating lessons suitable for their individual interests and abilities – a tall order perhaps, but an essential one.

Talents which go unrecognized

You might wonder whether it really matters if clever children go unrecognized as such during childhood. Why put so much effort into looking for clever children, when they'll probably come through alright by themselves?

The most obvious answer is that all children in Britain have the right to be educated according to their abilities. So leaving clever children to their own devices means failing them in that respect. Sometimes, clever children develop late because they were bored at school or their interests lay outside the school curriculum. Delius, the composer, showed no promise at Bradford Grammar School; neither Gandhi nor Nehru, the great Indian leaders, did well at school; Sarah Bernhardt, the actress, was expelled no less than three times.

Another important reason for seeking out clever children is that they usually find it difficult to develop their talents fully without some adult help. They need to be taught how to set about a subject. For example, they need to exercise their capacity for language, to develop a sense of the structure of foreign language and its literature, and to learn how to produce their best possible work.

Children whose minds are under-used often find ways of enduring boredom which can become bad habits, a hindrance throughout their lives. Paul Gauguin, the painter, took to daydreaming and seemed a slow thinker. Others become clever, restless nuisances like Lord Beaverbrook, who was a terror to everyone; St Francis of Assissi's father said he was a wild, impulsive boy. Some become 'butterfly thinkers', flitting from one new thing to another, always trying to find some satisfaction, when they could really do with some in-depth study (parents can encourage children to finish what they start). Children who are never able to use their abilities effectively can develop wrong images of themselves, thinking of themselves as being stupid or naughty, and because of that mistaken idea, they miss good career opportunities.

Eight-year-old Keith had this problem, but it took a long time to sort out. His mother had been blaming herself for his poor behaviour at school, while his teacher thought the boy was spoilt. But when I tested him and found that he had the potential to be brilliant, everything soon fell into place. His teacher gave him more difficult and interesting work at school, his parents encouraged him in more out-of-school activities, and with greater satisfaction, he quickly felt happier and behaved better.

Cleverness in children can be difficult for ordinary schools to cope with, as education is geared to the average youngster. After studying the lives of many eminent people one might conclude that they had achieved their success in spite of, rather than because of, their individual schools. Thomas Edison, the inventor, was taken out of school after the first three months because his teacher said he was 'unable'. Gregor Mendel, founder of the science of genetics, failed his teacher's exam four times and gave up trying for it after that. Isaac Newton, the great English physicist, left

159

school at fourteen and was sent back at nineteen because he read so much, but he later graduated from Cambridge without any distinction whatsoever. Yet for every success story about someone who did poorly in school, there's another of one who did well. Sometimes the education suits the child and sometimes it doesn't, so parents are still the child's best safeguard against educational disaster.

Generally speaking, education is a mass enterprise, arranged so that most children can benefit from it. But just as children of below average ability have difficulty in keeping up with the class, so clever children may have some trouble staying *back* with them.

What you can do – for problems at school

1 Watch out for signs that your child's being singled out as a 'show-off'. If she's really being forced to work below her natural level, talk to the headteacher about it. You may have to supplement her education or even move her to another school.

2 If your child finds it easy to reach the average for the class, try a little stretching. See if she can read a more advanced book, for example, or whether she can easily do more advanced mathematics. It may be that she'd be happier with a little more stimulation at home and at school.

3 If your child doesn't seem to be concentrating very well and you think that she is capable of it, try to find out whether she is spreading her talents too thinly or is unhappy.

4 Does your child's school make an effort to bring on the children's individual talents and interests? Don't let her individuality be lost in the attempt to fit in with the others. Watch out for sparks of interest and, if the school can't do anything for her, follow them up – without pressure – at home.

Watch out for your daughters

The poet who wrote 'Be good, sweet maid, and let who will

be clever' summed up some attitudes towards clever girls which are still around today. Though baby girls and boys do not start off with different aspirations, somehow the messages of what each should aim for seems to get through to them. Surveys of American students[3], for example, showed that in general girls were less keen to succeed in worldly terms than their brothers. They were also more likely to value a future occupation for the satisfaction it would bring them rather than for its possible money or status rewards. A report in the *Guardian*[4] from the UK Marriage Centre showed how, even in 1979, brides expected their paid work to take very low priority in their lives.

This lower expectation of success in girls takes shape as they grow and learn. It can eventually result in a poorer level of intellectual activity than they are capable of reaching. In school, girls are more modest about their abilities and achievements than boys, even when their results are exactly the same. As a result, they tend to attribute their school success to hard work, whereas boys say it's because they're clever. Boys often seem to have more confidence in their native ability than girls.

In America, a nationwide survey has found that many girls in mixed schools actually lower their goals so that the boys will like them more[5]. Even those girls who did come top of the class seemed to see it as some sort of 'mistake'. When they left school, they said they hadn't wanted to aim as high as they were capable of, because they thought they wouldn't be happy if they were 'too' clever. Many headmistresses of girls' schools in this country have claimed that the best chance of educational success a girl has is in an all-girls school. But doing well in particular subjects seems to vary from place to place. In Japan and Russia, for instance, where women's employment patterns are different, girls do relatively much better in science and maths than they do in the West.

Cleverness in girls seems to enhance their awareness of what is expected of their sex, which may be due to the extra sensitivity which very clever children seem to have. Highly intelligent girls can have particular problems due – even today – to conflicts between being clever and being feminine. So, when she reaches the age of eleven or twelve, it may seem easier for a girl to drop one of these supposedly conflicting aims. This lack of balance shows when she either becomes unduly concerned with traditionally feminine things, like making herself pretty, and does less than her best at school; or she may work extremely hard at school, setting very high standards for herself and seeming to despair if she does not always reach them. Clever girls can be very thin-skinned and over-react to this vulnerability by being bossy and domineering, sometimes at the expense of their qualities of imagination and creativity. So clever girls who do well at school may sometimes seem ruthlessly ambitious or insensitive – but this is really quite an untrue picture. Inside, they can be impatient and hungry for reassurance about everything, especially their femininity. Give them lots of praise, even (or specially) when they seem too big for their boots.

On the other hand, there are many more nice, clever little girls who sit quietly through lessons at school, demanding nothing and doing only as well as they're expected. If parents or teachers give them more difficult work they always rise to the occasion, showing that the ability is there, but it isn't often recognized since these girls don't claim enough attention for themselves. What often happens is that teachers see the boys as cleverer and give them the extra attention which brings them on further. Those who demand more are more likely to be spotted; parents should therefore watch out for this in their well-behaved little daughters.

What you can do – clever daughters

1   Ask your daughter how hard she finds her lessons. If she says they're easy, then she's probably intellectually under-exercised. Clever, obedient little girls need challenge, and are less likely to seek it out for themselves than boys are.

162

2   Talk to her teacher about it, if you think your daughter is only 'treading water' at school. The teacher will probably be glad you brought the situation to her notice, and together you can work out some way of getting your daughter to operate at her true level.

3   Treat your daughter in a way that respects her intelligence. Don't baby her, or underestimate her abilities. Try not to make too many assumptions. Let your son help with the ironing, for example, while your daughter changes the light bulb.

4   Help your daughter to explore her feelings about being clever and being a girl. Talk about school, what it means to her and how she expects to get on there and afterwards. Help her find her true interests, so that she can make the best career decisions when the time comes. It's never too early, since girls begin to get pushed in those directions considered appropriate to their sex from the time they're born.

5   Show your daughter successful women at work; if appropriate, her mother might be the best example. Point out how women can be doctors, not only nurses, and that maybe one day she'll be the first woman in her own field.

6   Be sure your encouragement for your daughter is real and that there aren't some secret hopes in your heart that one day she'll 'settle down' and make motherhood her only career. Many girls receive confusing messages like that when parents say 'Be a lawyer' with their mouths, but 'Be a housewife' with their tone.

What it's like to be clever

It's not much fun being different from your pals; you have to try extra hard to fit in if you want to stay friends with them. Children can be hard on outsiders, and clever children can be as hurt as any others when they feel left out.

All children are sensitive and need emotional support, but clever children sometimes seem to take this to an extreme.

They're exceptionally sensitive to criticism, especially from their friends. But at the same time they're often noticeably critical of others, not always an endearing characteristic. Such a child may need it pointed out to him gently, over and over again, that being right isn't all that matters. Sometimes he may be sure he's right about the rules of the game, and all the other players are wrong, but he has to learn that graciously giving way can be more appropriate than stamping off in disgust.

Clever children think particularly clearly, so they can often see or sense the right way of setting about things. They can pick out the most worthwhile ideas from a television programme, for example, and then wonder about different ways of ending it, whereas a less clever child may accept whatever comes on the screen without thinking much about it. The clever child wants to go on to discover more, which can sometimes lead her to dismiss out of hand what her teacher says and press on with her own ideas instead. Clever children thereby come up with crazy ideas sometimes, and if people react by laughing at them, it makes them feel a bit odd. The clever child asks herself 'Why can't they see what I mean?', but the adult realizes that a vital part of the child's knowledge is missing. It's like putting a jigsaw together without all the pieces.

When a clever child really gets down to something interesting, he hates to be interrupted. Even very tiny clever children are capable of concentrating so hard that they hear and see nothing else for hours. They want to go on and on until they're satisfied with the painting or the model they're making, so that interruptions to wash their hands at teatime can seem unbearable. Mother gets irritated and says to her four-year-old: 'But you've been playing with your soldiers for hours. It's time for tea now.' 'Just a minute, just a minute,' Brian mutters. Call follows call till his mother picks Brian up to do what she feels is right. Brian is frustrated and angry – kicks his heels – mother smacks – tears flow and a couple of black marks are chalked up, by Brian for the 'stupid' world he has to live in, and by mother for her 'stubborn' son.

Situations like this can appear in a flash. There was peace and suddenly there's chaos. Parents who know the ways of their clever children can, to some extent, avoid the build-up to this kind of problem. When you know that she's likely to settle down for an hour, make sure she doesn't start half an hour before tea. Explain to her in simple terms what's involved. Bargain with her if need be: 'If you start now, then you'll have to agree to break at four o'clock.' If this is all arranged beforehand, then a potentially damaging fight can be defused. But it means that parents have yet another burden of thinking ahead for their very special child.

Routine can be very irksome to a clever child. 'Why,' he may ask, 'do I always have to go to bed at six o'clock? It doesn't make sense; sometimes I'm not tired then.' There's nothing wrong with his logic; you will need to explain that parents have to have some time to themselves and that's why he has to amuse himself from six until he falls asleep. All children understand ideas of what's fair, so explain that you give him lots of time during the day and it's only fair if he gives you some to yourselves in the evening.

Balance

Clever children can be hard on parents, as they sometimes seem to exert a special kind of pressure on them. Parents may feel they're being sucked dry so that their own patience and concentration begins to wear thin. It's not that clever children are more demanding in the sense of wanting attention, but they're always trying out new ideas and challenging their parents' ways of thought, bringing about frequent tugs of war which are exhausting for everyone. The children know what they're doing and they can feel bad about wearing their parents out, but they do need the challenge of adult minds. Sometimes it's difficult for parents to accept that they're not as clever as their children, so they set up a sort of psychological rivalry with them, offering 'put-downs' instead of replies to questions by saying things such as: 'Surely you know that; I knew that when I was your age.' Watch out for this reaction in yourself and try to avoid it. Answer questions as well as you can or say honestly: 'I don't know; let's find out.' The path to good communication between parents and clever children is always smoothed with honesty.

The clever child's extra quick ability to take things in and size up situations can be a burden to her. It can bring her pain as well as pleasure. Such children sometimes use their clever, intellectual minds as a shield to protect their emotional sensitivity, but this can get out of hand. Jasmine was brought to see me by her mother when she was only eight years old because, although she was always top of the class at school and was extremely well behaved, she wasn't happy. Jasmine had some idea of what was happening to herself; she felt empty inside, phoney, dead and cut-off from herself. She seemed to be not just clever, but to have lost herself in her intellectual life so that she couldn't reach out to other people any more or form close ties with other children. This had made her feel bad about herself and unhappy.

Jasmine had filled up her emptiness by collecting more and more knowledge – she had a passion for reading and memorizing encyclopaedias – but her imagination was beginning to suffer. For example, her stamp collection was superb, but she didn't even wonder about the lives of the people who lived in the countries whose names she knew so well. Her parents were very proud of Jasmine's school success, with good reason, but sometimes the pride took over their description of their daughter to such an extent that they seemed to be living through her. Jasmine didn't seem to mind and even went along with it, evidently enjoying living out her parents' own hopes.

But Jasmine's load was becoming too heavy for her eight-year-old shoulders. She still had babyish parts of herself deep inside which were hungry for attention; she needed more love for herself and less for her cleverness. Her real, more fragile self needed a boost – somehow she was being robbed of her childhood and felt that she had to go on being clever to win her parents' love.

We talked a lot about it; the problem wasn't really obstinate. Jasmine, her parents and myself (the psychologist) soon began to realize what was happening in her life, and we found some ways to ease the situation. Her parents stopped themselves from over-praising her success at school (at least in front of her) and offered more praise for her newly developing friendliness and openness. They told her how much she meant to them and gave her more hugs and kisses than they had done. It was a bit hard at first, as all the family had become a bit stiff and embarrassed about that sort of thing, but it soon began to work. Jasmine made heroic efforts to be less of an intellectual snob at school; catching herself seeing the other children as stupid, she began to be able to look on them as friends, which was much nicer.

Jasmine is thirteen years old now and coming up to adolescence, a child changing to a young woman. Her teachers are pressing her to do well in her exams for the honour of the school (and she probably will, too), but she's on a much firmer emotional base now, so that she can cope better with all the pressures of a normal teenager. It took some concern, some thinking and feeling through and a lot of effort, but Jasmine's not going to grow up as an unbalanced woman, all brains and no feelings, and it was well worth it. She's happy now.

What you can do – for a balanced life

1   Avoid problem build-up by making sure a clever child has enough time to work and feel satisfied by what he achieves. Try not to cut him short if you can help it.

2   Use reason with a clever child, more perhaps than with other children, as that's what they're good at. Explain what you're trying to do with honesty, talk about feelings – his and other peoples' – so that he learns to see himself as part of a working group, the family.

3 If your clever child seems to be taking more of your attention than you can afford, take a break if you can. You don't have to be on duty non-stop! Even a two-year-old can be left for a short while when he's, say, working on a jigsaw. He should be able to understand that you need to lie down or do something else for a while; you're there all right, but not at his beck and call. Parents of clever children have to learn how to relax instantly when the moment arrives!

4 Emphasize that there's more to life than doing well at school. To be mentally active may mean understanding others, for example, or thinking up ways to help others. Being clever is more than an ability to do maths.

Chapter 8

EDUCATING CLEVER CHILDREN

This chapter brings together some of the most important new knowledge about the educational needs of clever children. Until recently, concern has been centred on providing good education for the average child so that it has seemed undemocratic to offer anything different for exceptionally clever children. Interest is growing now, though, in the education of our brightest, most talented and most skilled young citizens. As a result, more information about the type of education they need is coming together from many sources around the world.

Your home as a learning centre

It's the little everyday things that can make all the difference to your happiness and success in bringing up a clever child. A sensible move is to try to get your house organized right from the beginning so that it's a lived-in, but efficient place for learning and leaves you with the greatest possible amount of time to devote to your child. Here are some thoughts and ideas which you can adapt to your own circumstances.

Homes where little children are growing and learning are usually a mess. There are paints and toys, bits of paper, cushions and all sorts of things which they need handy for daily living, but which don't do much for the decor. Take it easy; it's like that for everyone who hasn't got a nanny to supervise the nursery. For some years, it is very likely that that is the way it's going to be, so don't make constant efforts to keep the place perfectly in order. It only frays everyone's nerves and can slow up the children's learning when, for example, they can't cut up pieces of paper without a scolding. If you would like a nice area to be alone in, or for entertaining your friends – and who doesn't – then make a space just for parents. This is most usually the 'front room', which can quite easily be forbidden to children.

A stimulating home is gay, colourful and probably noisy. There are pictures on the walls, ornaments and things to handle. Music is also important; not just the background 'muzak' interspersed with chatter which comes over the radio for hours, but real sit-down, pay-attention bursts of something you all enjoy. A sense of rhythm helps children to speak early and to develop in a more balanced way.

When your child is old enough to draw, make sure his efforts go up on the wall, and in important places too – not just in the kitchen. Mount them simply, as many primary schools do, on thick cardboard with a thick felt tip line ruled around, so that they're shown to their best advantage. You'll all get a lot of pleasure and pride from looking at them. You can attach them with something like Blu-Tak, as the mounts can be used again. Change them from time to time so that he is encouraged to do more – it shows your respect and appreciation of his efforts. But if he hasn't got to that stage yet – stick posters or pictures of your own up.

All children should have a place for their own books right from the start. It doesn't have to be a smart bookcase, as long as it is somewhere the child knows she can go and find something to read. Buy her a new book from time to time, especially if you think she's ready to move on with her reading. Each child in the family should have her own supply of books which are hers alone so that she can learn to care for them and use them in her own way. The book area should be attractive and the books stored not too close together, so that podgy little fingers can get hold of them easily.

For the same reasons it's better for children to have a special place for their toys. It should be big and reachable enough to make a child's clearing-up job easy, so that the mess can be kept to a reasonable level. If he has to put things carefully one on top of another in his cupboard, he'll be less inclined to take that trouble and will either ignore his instructions or jumble things in anyhow and maybe break them.

Keep messy and water play strictly to kitchen and bathroom so that your child can have a great time splashing and learning about the properties of water without fear of a telling-off. If you let him trail around, you'll all suffer from the stains and their consequences.

The material that children use for learning is important, and there should be plenty of it. You will need lots of sharpened pencils, felt tip pens, paints and paper. Wallpaper lining is handy at first, then older children can move to drawing paper, bought in bulk. Children need scissors and paste, and nowadays paste comes in solid form so there need not be quite the sticky mess there always was when my own children were small. Be lavish but not profligate with materials. It's part of their learning process that children should appreciate value.

Junk has its uses, as every primary school teacher knows. Egg boxes, lavatory rolls, jam jars and so on are the stock-in-trade of the learning child. They're the basis of a thousand imaginative models. Add to that beans, seeds, shells, fir cones, wrapping paper, cloth etc – the supply is endless and virtually free. Keep a special overall handy for a child to work in and be sure his wet-work overall is waterproof.

Children have to clear up. Be firm, give them warnings and plenty of time, but you must supervise. Even a two-year-old can make a good job of it, with a little help from Mummy or Daddy. Encourage children to help each other so that it doesn't matter who made what mess; otherwise, you could spend a good deal of time in argument. If there's a real reluctance, start by handing out simple tasks, such as 'John, please put your pencils in this box so that I can put it in the cupboard.' Don't nag; be specific, and give lots of praise where it's due.

Play

There is something about the way clever children enjoy learning that can give parents the impression that playing is, for them, a waste of time. Clever children can seem miniature adults with their knowing ways and lively minds, so that play does not seem to be a valuable part of their lives, and parents may believe that their child does not need to play. But to think of play as a useless activity, and encourage the child only to do more school-type work such as reading, would take away some of the richness of life as a child. It can be taken as a rule of child development that even the most sophisticated and mature child still needs to play.

The value of play is not only in the amusement and relaxation it gives a child, but also for the learning it provides. This learning is both emotional and intellectual. Emotionally, even a toddler can play out aspects of his life which he does not quite understand, so that he becomes more familiar with what's going on and finds it easier to live with. Intellectually, play lets a child take in new information and manipulate it to fit in with what he knows already. Through play a child can practise and improve his thinking and the development of his creativity. Play with other children is a very valuable means of learning social and communication skills, especially for children who have a tendency to be solitary.

As well as everyday play, which children enjoy and which they have worked out themselves, parents can make suggestions for play. Playgroups and nursery schools offer their charges directed play with the sand and water they provide and the activities the children do together. Here are a few ideas for parents at home which offer some mental exercise:

* Have your three-year-old imagine she's a robot. Then let her work out what effect this would have on the world if it were really true. Encourage her to think about how robots would change the way we live today and what sort of help it would be able to give with our daily chores. You can broaden this idea further over the years to take in all sorts of imaginary technical inventions.

* Next time your toddler piles up his blocks into a tall and

shaky tower, talk to him about it. See if he can imagine what would happen if he put a bigger block on top, or a smaller one. Then get him to try out his 'hypothesis' – using the smaller block first. Perhaps, by some judicious questions and suggestions, you could work his mind round to the idea that some blocks can act to support the tower (buttresses). This sort of play helps to teach problem-solving skills.

* A clever four-year-old can have a lot of fun thinking up her own games, rather than just following the rules of those she knows already. Suggest to her that she makes up a game, with her own rules, using something she's interested in – like a set of her favourite toy animals – then try out the game with the other children she plays with.

Learning at school

The key to providing suitable education for clever children in schools lies in more flexible methods of teaching; these are being used in something like half our primary schools, but are barely filtering into the secondary schools. For example, team teaching is now frequently used in primary schools. Each teacher is a member of a team who look after several classes of children. The members of the team have their own special talents which are then offered to all the children in their group, providing them with a much broader approach to learning than they would have had with only one teacher and with variety, too, which is an antidote to drudgery.

Infant schools often use the village school system which cuts out the gradation of children by age. So five-, six- and seven-year-olds will be in the same class, just as they used to be in village schools. The older ones can then take care of the younger ones, guiding them in school lore and helping them tie their shoelaces and put their coats on. It gives the older ones a sense of responsibility and takes away the fear of school from the newcomers. It also reduces competition for places in the class and allows the children to work at their own pace – slow or fast.

My suggestion is a football team approach. Just as groups

of the school's most talented footballers might gather together on Saturday mornings or after school for a practice under the games master, so should clever children have the same provision for their mental skills. They could be taken in buses to join up with other schools to form a bigger group. The facilities are there in all the schools and it would not cost much to keep them open for just a little longer. Such sessions should be open to all who want them; those who lost interest would soon drop out.

All of these ideas, and others, can break up the lock-step of rigid formal teaching where each child is locked by age or school class into the same lessons, timing and homework regardless of his ability and maturity. Thinking around the problem can help to provide clever children with the varied stimulation and regular challenge they need in school. For that matter, such ideas can be used to improve education for all children.

But in the more conventional, age-graded systems used by most schools, parents and teachers have to work within the structure. One obvious choice in this situation is for the child to jump a class if she's very bright. This seems to be easier for both the child and school to cope with in the earliest years of education. Alternatively, a child in a really flexible school (whose headteacher is a wizard at timetables) might skip a class in just one or two subjects. This is more likely to happen in secondary schools where subjects are treated separately with different teachers and specific times alloted to them. Clever children coming to the end of their school careers may be able to join in on some college lectures in subject areas in which they excel.

If a child is likely to move up to a class of children a year or two older than himself, either for a little while or permanently, parents should pay particular attention to the following three points:
* Has he really got the physical ability to take part in games and activities with older children? If he hasn't, he may begin to think of himself as a 'weed', a physical and (maybe)

174

mental failure. His teachers may soon forget his real age and may confirm these unfortunate feelings he has about himself by calling him, say, a 'little' boy.

* Has she got the mental ability to play with older children on equal terms? If she's always the youngest in the group, and she behaves like it, then the others are likely to exclude her from their play and it may make her feel bad.

* Is he socially mature enough to cope with being with older children all the school day? It takes quite a lot of effort to behave older than you really are for eight hours a day, five days a week. Would it be fair to place that strain on your child for his entire school life?

Usually, even for very bright children, it isn't the best idea for them to be jumped a class. It's often much better to try to provide them with something extra to work at, either in school or out of school hours.

Private education

About six parents in every hundred send their children to private schools in Britain. Why do they choose to pay? When parents were asked in a British survey[1] why they had chosen the private sector, they replied that they had two main expectations from private schools:

* to give their children a better chance of exam success
* to direct their children towards sharing the same feelings and outlook on life as they did. In other words, they felt their children would be more likely to behave in the way the parents wanted.

Parents who could afford it but who are undecided about whether to send their children to state or private schools should be sure of what they're thinking of buying. For example, they may tend to prefer a private school because they feel that the classes will be smaller and so their child will get more personal attention. This may be true on average, but individual schools differ: big private schools, especially secondary schools, have the same class sizes (about thirty) as state schools, but either type of school may take smaller groups of children for some lessons. Parents should ask exactly how the school's teaching groups are arranged. The alternative may be to move to a catchment area for the state school you prefer – if you can.

The teachers in private schools are often assumed to be of a 'higher standard', but, in fact, all teachers are awarded their qualifications by the state system in Britain so the difference in the actual quality of their teaching is not likely to be great. However, teachers do naturally apply for posts in schools where they feel most comfortable, and so the kind of teachers who end up in private schools are more likely to meet with the approval of the schools' clients – the parents. During my own research I questioned teachers about their educational aims and, on exmaining the evidence, I found that there was no real difference between those in state or private schools. In general they're not happy about compromising their educational beliefs, whatever these may be, whoever pays their salaries.

In our immensely varied educational system, every school has to be judged on its own merits. Parents want all sorts of different things for their children, and only they know what these are. So it is important when looking at a school not to take anything for granted. The standard of teaching, the atmosphere, the size of the classes, individual attention, physical punishment, emphasis on sport, etc – these can all affect the present and future life of your child, whether the school is state or private.

The idea of the old eleven-plus exam was that clever children should be selected for special education in the grammar schools, unencumbered by the needs of less clever children, who were sent to secondary modern or technical schools. One of the main reasons this is being dismantled is that the selection of children was found to be both unreliable and unfair. There were other problems about the eleven-plus exam, too, which apply just as much to children going to any schools which select their pupils by an exam. For example, children who are told they're better or worse than other children soon begin to think of themselves in that way, so children who pass the exam to the selective schools often feel superior while those who don't feel themselves to be failures. Well, that's life, you may say, but it does bring many problems for the children which weren't there before selection.

Selective schools sometimes offer a very limited, lop-sided form of education dedicated to getting most of their pupils through public exams. It teaches them to think in a compartmentalized way which hampers creativity. There is more pressure on the children to be successful in exam terms, which can be too much for some, giving them emotional problems. But on the other hand, clever children can be very happy at selective schools. They rub shoulders with children who are as bright as they are and who are as keen to do well. They're unlikely to suffer from a lot of boredom because the lessons are pitched at their own level and parents are usually very involved with what they're doing at school. As you might expect, selective schools do get better exam results than mixed-ability schools – after all, the pupils are pre-selected for their cleverness – though the teaching methods are usually pretty conventional.

Many human aptitudes, though, are better developed outside the classroom than in it. Clever children, who can sometimes become over-intellectual, can benefit greatly through contact and working with artists, performers, agricultural and industrial scientists, scholars, craftsmen and other professionals who are not necessarily educators. As parents, you could suggest that the school makes arrangements with local colleges for those pupils who could benefit from it, of all ages, to go to a few classes, attend a course, or meet some of the lecturers for discussion.

It's not ideas that are lacking, nor even money. The educational provision for clever children can be improved to a considerable extent within the facilities we already have. It needs a fresh outlook, a real concern, a willingness to tinker with routine, to think sideways, Clever children need adult energy to help them now, for one day we will benefit from theirs.

What children really want from school

In my research (outlined on page 153) I asked over 200 clever children, aged from five to fifteen, what they wanted from their education, and most of them were clear about what that was. In general, what they wanted was a change of approach – in the style of education rather than the content. They did not want to be set aside for lessons and made to seem different from their comrades, but they did suggest some changes which could be of value to clever children. This is how they answered.

What kind of lessons do you like?

The preferred lessons were long ones, where the clever children felt they had time to really get to grips with what they were doing. They didn't like little snippets of information being handed out to them. They liked to see the pattern of learning they were using; for example, a twelve-year-old boy said he was interested in the principles of heat production, but he'd had to spend a lot of time learning facts first. He felt he should have had had the two aspects together.

The clever children wanted to be able to take part in designing their own lessons. Teachers don't always outline the syllabus to pupils, but the clever children wanted to know what they were supposed to be aiming for and how they were to spend their time getting there. They would like to devise their own routes sometimes, too. A girl of thirteen said her teacher often gave the class lists to memorize in history, which she found very frustrating; she'd really have benefitted more from a broader approach to the problems of the period she was studying, such as an understanding of the era and then the filling in of details.

What do you think education should do for you?

Clever children saw their education as helping them to grow up to be well balanced and competent. They wanted their own values and interests to be respected while they were at school, and seemed to resent what they described as an over-emphasis on their intellectual cleverness which was shown in

178

the approval and praise they were given for passing exams with top marks. A word often used by the children was 'healthy' – they wanted a 'healthy' education.

Are you ever bored?
All children have moments of boredom in school, but clever children's boredom was often due to the special ways they have of learning, which teachers weren't always aware of. For example, for most children learning a subject usually progresses from simple to complex, singular to plural, and in the 'right' order – right according to the school, that is. But clever children sometimes skip bits of the process, so that while the teacher is explaining how to do long-division in the time-honoured manner, the clever child has worked it out long ago. That's the point at which the clever child becomes bored or impatient. Flexible methods of teaching can help here, so that a few children don't have to wait in silence and stillness for the rest to catch up; when children work at their own pace, time is not wasted in waiting. The clever children often said that if they were able to explore their own way more – under guidance – they wouldn't be bored. A fifteen-year-old boy said he felt over-controlled at school; he was keen to get on with the subjects that interested him, but he had to learn only what the teachers told him.

A few children said they were bored because it was all too easy. They longed for a really testing situation, with other children who were up to their level and who might even challenge them to failure. A group of clever girls used to meet outside school hours to discuss ideas which their teachers felt weren't suitable for the class.

What kind of teacher do you like?
Overall, the clever children wanted teachers to teach – even the five-year-olds. Friendly, warm-hearted teachers were nice to be with, but these children had a thirst for knowledge which went beyond that, and where better to get it than from teachers? The most sought-after teachers were not the

cleverest, though, but the most open-minded. The brighter the child, the less likely he was to be affected by the teacher's personality or style of teaching, and the more independent the child's learning. The combination of a flexible school and an open-minded teacher, secure in herself, is a sure-fire winner in clever children's eyes.

How should schools be run?
The clever children came up with some ingenious ideas. Some were concerned with mundane things like school dinners, but others took administration seriously. For example, several children suggested that having a single headteacher was undemocratic; there should be a group of teachers at the top with pupil participation at all levels to make the school work at its best. In general the brighter the child, the more independent of the 'system' they seemed to be. They put up with it (whatever it was) while they had to, but when they got the power they really intended to change things.

Get involved with the school
It's very important for the parents of clever children to keep in really close communication with their children while they're going to school, from the earliest days. Parents have to be actively working with children and their teachers to get the best results, and there isn't a better person to ask about a clever child's educational needs than the child herself at any age.

Try the following suggestions for talking points about school. They are the sort of concerns which might not come up during tea-table conversation, but which might ease your child's school life if they're approached directly.
* Are his special interests being catered for at all?
* Has he any particular problems?
* How are these problems being tackled?
* What are the really satisfying experiences that happen at school?

180

* What sort of learning does he prefer?
* What progress is he making at school in different subject areas?
* What could you recommend to (or talk over with) teachers or other parents?

What you can do – with the school

1   Talk with the teacher about the way your child seems to be getting on there.
2   Ask about the possibility of there being something extra in the basic day's teaching for children like yours.
3   Talk about ways in which your child's interests can be developed at school so that she can perhaps specialize to some extent.
4   Talk about ways in which her horizons might be broadened so that she develops new interests.
5   See where she can share these new possibilities of learning with others in the class.
6   Don't try to push the teacher to give a lot of attention to your child's special interests when she may feel that, for example, her writing is a matter of priority. She does need good basic skills too.
7   Don't expect your child to be as enthusiastic as you may be over all aspects of her education.

Good co-operation between school and home is usually the case, but there are exceptions, when parents and teachers just do not seem to be on the same wavelength. In my study, which involved sixty-one primary and secondary schools in the North of England, headteacher-parent relationships could sometimes have been improved upon. In nearly a third of the schools, for example, there was no formal parent-teacher set-up at all. Contact with class teachers often had to be made, in those schools, through the school secretary with the head's permission. This is a rather inhibiting procedure if you merely want to talk about something that's bothering you, or if you want to get to know the teacher's approach better. Half the headteachers said that parents should have no say at all in the running of the school and about a third would have refused extra educational help for their brightest pupils – if it had been offered.

Extra education outside school

When parents have particular educational interests and the headteacher is either too overloaded with work or is not interested in that area, in order to be effective in promoting it parents have to act outside the school's influence. Those who believe that their children are in need of extra educational help, because they are very bright, may choose to pool their resources to give their children what they can. You can form your own group of active parents, providing a broader and deeper education for your children. But before doing anything, it might be wise to write to:

The National Association for Gifted Children
1 South Audley Street
London W1 5DQ
(Tel: 01-499 1188 or 1189)

The association is a registered charity which has lots of experience of all sorts of clever children and runs courses and holidays for them. They can put you in touch with your local branch, if there is one, or help you start one.

Setting up a parents' group

If you want your group to be a more intimate and local one, below are some suggestions of how to go about setting one up:

* The parents who start it should be those who have the time and energy to stay with the project and see it through.

* Form a committee made up of concerned parents, teachers or other people in the community. Select a temporary chairperson, to get the ball rolling, and sort out a plan of action. Then start with a meeting in someone's house to organize your group better. Have a theme which someone will speak on with a discussion to follow. Keep a record of suggestions for activities and needs which are made at the meeting.

* Let tact be the order of the day. Keep the school informed

182

and involved as far as you can while you're getting settled. Ask them for help such as contacting other parents who may be interested. The school is more than likely to be on your side; after all, you're all after the educational welfare of the children. Ask parents who are interested to sign a list and to suggest others.

* Divide up the chores into sub-groups. For example, you should have people specifically in charge of finance, programme, community resources, liaison or special needs. Someone with legal knowledge can be very useful too. Decide how much you'll need to cover your expenses so that you can charge a non-profit making membership fee. Perhaps the school would help out here. Decide on a contact address, which doesn't change, so that newcomers can join in easily.

The following are the sort of things your group could do:
* Have parent education meetings, either listening to experts or trying out educational projects with your children.
* Compile a newsletter, in which the children take part, and which circulates ideas of interest.
* Establish where the local resources, such as special library facilities, are to be found.
* Organize field trips for parents and children, preferably with someone who can talk about the subject of the visit.
* Talk with and counsel each other; discuss problems in common.

What you can do – for your clever child

Here are some of the most important ideas from this book, which you may find useful as a check list on your own family situation.

1   A child is always a child. When your five-year-old has made remarkable progress, take pride in it. But please remember that he's still only had five years of life and experience, so he needs comforting when he cuts his finger or can't zip up his jacket, as well as information to answer his complex questions.

2   Relax and take pleasure in your clever one. Sometimes her great stamina and persistence may get you down. But catch on to her excitement in learning – it more than makes up for your fatigue.·

3   Keep close to your child. Listen and talk to him – communication between parents and children is vital from birth, so it's never too early to start. Don't put it off until you've got time; there's no time like the present, and it may not wait. Let the telephone ring sometimes. It's probably less important than whatever he has to tell you.

4   Don't boast about your clever child – comparing her with other children you know – especially not in front of her. It puts the clever child into a position where she has to live up to what you say about her or else let you down. Nor is it justified as far as other children are concerned; every child is an individual, and unfavourable comparison is unpleasant for anyone concerned. Wholesome pride is another matter, though.

5   Try to keep your child's life active and interesting most of the time. Go out and about as a family as much as you can; let him meet anyone interesting who comes to your house; go to concerts or on walks together. Keep a changing supply of books and newspapers in the house, and talk about what's in them. Try cooking together, for example, using a recipe book.

6   Encourage your child to fulfil herself in whatever she's interested in. It can be tiresome for parents to be involved in the same topic of conversation, such as prehistoric monsters, over and over again, but work on it with her. Sort out a library research system together; keep notes and arrange your findings so that the extra learning can be a lot of fun too. By the time she's ·exhausted her enthusiasm for dinosaurs, she'll be much more competent to tackle her next enthusiasm – perhaps for collecting shells.

7   Let children just *be* when they want to. Don't drive

them to distraction with things to do every minute of every day. Children need time to collect their thoughts and feelings, do nothing or 'waste time' just like adults. For balance and peace of mind everyone needs time to stand and stare. Let your clever child daydream if he wants to, lying on an unmade bed and staring at the ceiling. Clever children should play, too; just like other children they need their quota of fun.

8   Try to help your child to find her own interests, rather than fulfilling *your* ambitions, or forcing on her what you think is suitable for her age or sex. 'Meet my child, the doctor' isn't always a joke. Clever children are often good at many things, and it's hard to sort out what they'd especially like to do. So help them try their hands at different things – like chemistry, carpentry, pottery or organizing things. A clever child may know which direction she wants to aim in; your job is to guide and help her get there, over the problems on the way. She'll do best and be happiest at what she really wants to do.

9   Give your child praise for doing well, but also praise him for trying to do well. Things sometimes seem so easy for clever children that parents forget to praise their efforts. But they need your approval as much as any other child. Combine your praise with suggestions sometimes; clever children appreciate that too. Enquiring minds have to take intellectual risks, but they need the safety net of knowing that your support is always there.

10 Being clever is no reason for a child to be badly behaved – far from it. Clever children are quicker at picking up the family rules and also at knowing what to do in the outside world. Don't make excuses for anti-social behaviour, such as when she screams for chocolate in the supermarket, by saying: 'Well, she's so clever it's difficult for her to cope with life.' It really isn't any more difficult for her than it is for any other child.

11 Be there when he needs you – the cleverest and most independent little boy needs a helping hand sometimes –

185

but stand back and let him take the lead at other times. Knowing when to take action and when not to is a matter of sensitivity. You have to judge each moment as it arrives.

12 Let your child see in you the qualities you'd like her to have. If it's a case of do as I say, not as I do – then clever children will see through you and go their own way. Don't tell her to read while you're watching television, for example; it doesn't make sense to a clever child, and such an attitude can cause great ill-feeling between you.

13 Try to keep an atmosphere of respect for learning in your home and encourage the quest for knowledge. There's no need to go overboard, though – you can teach your child to keep a wary eye open for opinion masquerading as information. Even books can be wrong!

14 There's a difference between pushing a child and encouraging him to make a little extra effort. Somehow, we can't see this pushing in ourselves, but can easily spot it in other parents. Perhaps your children can tell you whether they feel pushed or encouraged; they'll know.

15 Keep good relations with your child's school. Support their efforts as well as you can. Although you may disagree with your child's teacher, don't belittle her in front of the child. Explain privately how your opinions differ, and try to find ways of working together.

16 Be as aware as you can of your own feelings as the parents of a clever child. Watch out for feelings of jealousy or competition. See that there aren't any 'putdowns' in your conversations with her, and that there's a sincere desire on your part to be a supportive parent. Sometimes jealous feelings can grow in parents when children are very clever; these can lead to over-protection and exploitation of the child's talents to the detriment of her psychological well being.

17 Keep children as clear of labels and categories as you can; labels can be false, and often stick. Your son may

be 'clever', and he may be 'shy' sometimes, but he's always William to you, and so he should be to his teacher.

18 Try not to act like a parent all the time, feeling that your way is always best. Allow your child a lot of liberty on unimportant issues, so that she can work things out in her own way whenever possible.

19 When there's a problem over discipline, talk things out with your child if possible. Clever children are much better able to listen to reason than ordinary children, and they usually have a well-developed sense of duty.

20 Don't expect your child to be clever all the time. That kind of halo makes for a bad headache.

References

Chapter 1   The Clever Ones
1   Anne Roe (1952), 'The Psychologist Examines 64 Eminent Scientists'. *Scientific American, 187,* pp.21-25.
2   Eleanor E. Maccoby and C. Jacklin (1974), *The Psychology of Sex Differences.* Stanford: Stanford University Press.
3   Joan Freeman (1979), *Gifted Children: Their identification and development in a social context.* Lancaster: MTP Press.

Chapter 2   Your Amazing Baby
1   J.H. Kennell, D.K. Voos and M.H. Klaus (1979), 'Parent-infant bonding', in J.D. Osafsky (ed.), *Handbook of Infant Development.* New York: Wiley.
2   Y. Brackbill (1979), 'Obstetrical medication and infant behaviour', in J.D. Osafsky (ed.), *Handbook of Infant Development.* New York: Wiley.
3   Michael Lewis (ed.) (1976), *Origins of Intelligence.* London: Wiley.

Chapter 3   The Making of Minds
1   Joan Freeman (1981, 2nd edition), *Human Biology and Hygiene.* Oxford: Pergamon Press.
2   Robert E. Ornstein (1972, *The Psychology of Consciousness.* New York: Viking Press.
3   H.J. Eysenck and Leon Kamin (1981), *Intelligence: The battle for the mind.* London: Pan Paperbacks.
4   A.R. Jensen (1972), *Genetics and Education.* London: Methuen.
5   David Lewis (1981), *You Can Teach Your Child Intelligence.* London: Souvenir Press.
6   J. Newson and E. Newson (1979), *Toys and Playthings.* Harmondsworth: Penguin.
7   Jean Marzollo (1980), *Supertot: A parents' guide to toddlers.* London: George Allen and Unwin.

8   William J.J. Gordon (1981), *SES Creative Sampler*. Cambridge, Massachusetts: SES Associates.

Chapter 4   Growing Up Clever

1   Joan Tough (1973), *Focus on Meaning: Talking to some purpose with young children*. London: George Allen and Unwin.

2   J.B.W. Douglas (1964), *The Home and School*. London: Panther.

3   Department of Education and Science (1967), *Children and Their Primary Schools* (The Plowden Report).

4   G.W. Brown and T. Harris (1978), *The Social Origins of Depression*. London: Tavistock.

5   R. Rapoport, R. Rapoport and Z. Strelitz (1977), *Fathers, Mothers and Others*. London: Routledge and Kegan Paul.

6   Eleanor E. Maccoby and C. Jacklin (1974), *The Psychology of Sex Differences*. Stanford: Stanford University Press.

7   Mary Stewart (1962), *The Success of the First-born Child*. Worker's Educational Association.

8   L. Belmont and F.A. Marolla (1973), 'Birth order, family size and intelligence'. *Science, 182,* pp.1096-1101.

9   B. Sutton-Smith and B.G. Rosenberg (1970), *The Siblings*. New York: Holt, Rinehart and Winston.

10   A. Lawson and J.D. Ingleby (1974), 'Daily routines of pre-school children: effects of age, birth order, sex and social class'. *Psychological Medicine, 4*, pp.399-415.

11   M.P.M. Richards (1977), 'An ecological study of infant development in an urban setting in Britain', in P.H. Leiderman, S.R. Tulkin and A. Rosenfield (eds.), *Culture and Infancy*. New York: Academic Press.

12   M. Rutter, D. Quinton and W. Yule (1976), *Family Pathology and Disorder in the Children*. London: Wiley.

Chapter 5   The Three Rs

1   M.M. Clark (1976), *Young Fluent Readers*. London: Heinemann Educational.

2   Glenn Doman (1965), *Teach Your Baby to Read*. London: Jonathan Cape.

3   Susan Hampshire (1980), *Susan's Story*. London: Sidgwick and Jackson.
4   Joan Dean and Ruth Nichols (1974), *Framework for Reading*. London: Evans Brothers.

Chapter 6   Early Success at School
1   H.F. Harlow (1969), 'Age-mate or peer affectional system', in D.S. Lerhman, R.A. Hinde and E. Shaw (eds.), *Advances in the Study of Behaviour,* Vol 2, pp.333-383. New York: Academic Press.
2   Trades Union Congress Working Party (1976), *The Under Fives*. London: TUC.
3   Jerome Bruner (1980), *Under Five in Britain*. London: Grant McIntyre.
4   Emlyn Williams (1956), *The Corn is Green*. London: Heinemann Educational.
5   M. Rutter, N. Maughan, P. Mortimore and J. Ouston (1979), *Fifteen Thousand Hours*. London: Open Books.
6   V.H. Goertzel and M.G. Goertzel (1962), *Cradles of Eminence*. Boston: Little, Brown & Co.
7   Tony Buzan (1974), *Use Your Head*. London: BBC Publications.

Chapter 7   Too Clever by Half
1   Joan Freeman (1979), *Gifted Children: Their identification and development in a social context*. Lancaster: MTP Press.
2   Eric Ogilvie (1973), *Gifted Children in Primary Schools*. London: Macmillan.
3   C.P. Smith (ed.), *Achievement Related Motives in Children*. New York: Russell Sage Foundation.
4   Penny Mansfield (1982), 'With stars in their eyes and a wife at the sink'. Report from the UK Marriage Centre (reported in the *Guardian*).
5   J.S. Coleman (1961), *The Adolescent Society*. Glencoe, N Y.: Free Press

Chapter 8   Educating Clever Children
1   Tessa Bridgeman and Irene Fox (1978), 'Why people choose private schools'. *New Society, 44*, pp.702-705.

Suggested Reading

Your Exceptional Child by Brian Jackson (Fontana, 1980).
An affectionate introduction to the idea that children are different and some are clever.

The Developing Child by Helen Bee (Harper and Row, 1978).
More of a textbook, but written clearly, giving a wide picture of the recognized stages of development.

Framework for Reading by Joan Dean and Ruth Nichols (Evans Brothers, 1974).
Written for teachers, but provides the clear essential steps to take in helping a child to learn to read.

Focus on Meaning by Joan Tough (George Allen and Unwin, 1973).
A detailed guide on how to talk to children with some purpose.

Gifted Children by Joan Freeman (MTP Press, 1979).
Offers a broad look at the way clever children can be seen by others, and the ways in which they react to this in their families.

Intelligence: The Battle for the Mind by Hans Eysenck and Leon Kamin (Pan, 1981).
A lively debate on the IQ tests measure.

Toys and Playthings by John and Elizabeth Newson (Penguin, 1979).
A warm-hearted general look at the myriad ways in which children play with whatever they have to hand.

Supertot by Jean Marzollo (George Allen and Unwin, 1980).
A constant source of activities for active toddlers.

Teaching Clever Children 7-11 by Norman Tempest (Routledge and Kegan Paul, 1974).
A lively report on an experimental teaching scheme used in Southport, and what seemed to work.

Children's Minds by Margaret Donaldson (Fontana, 1978).
A carefully thought out picture of mental development from different points of view.